H TO WOW

YOUR CHURCH GUESTS

101 WAYS
to make a meaningful first impression

MARK L. WALTZ

Group

Loveland, Colorado

group.com

Group resources really work!

This Group resource incorporates our R.E.A.L. approach to ministry. It reinforces a growing friendship with Jesus, encourages long-term learning, and results in life transformation, because it's

Relational
Learner-to-learner interaction enhances learning and builds Christian friendships.

Experiential
What learners experience through discussion and action sticks with them up to 9 times longer than what they simply hear or read.

Applicable
The aim of Christian education is to equip learners to be both hearers and doers of God's Word.

Learner-based
Learners understand and retain more when the learning process takes into consideration how they learn best.

HOW TO WOW YOUR CHURCH GUESTS

101 ways to make a meaningful first impression

Copyright © 2011 Mark L. Waltz
Visit our website: **group.com**

This book was edited and designed by the stellar team at Group Publishing.

All Scripture quotations, unless otherwise indicated, are taken from the Holy Bible, New International Version®, NIV®. Copyright © 1973, 1978, 1984 by Biblica, Inc.™ Used by permission of Zondervan. All rights reserved worldwide. www.zondervan.com

Library of Congress Cataloging-in-Publication Data
Waltz, Mark L.
  How to wow your church guests : 101 ways to make a meaningful first impression / Mark L. Waltz.
    p. cm.
  ISBN 978-0-7644-6991-6 (pbk. : alk. paper)
  1. Hospitality--Religious aspects--Christianity. 2. Interpersonal
relations--Religious aspects--Christianity. 3. Church greeters. 4.
Church marketing. 5. Church growth. I. Title.
  BV4647.H67W35 2011
  253--dc23
                                2011018849

ISBN 978-0-7644-6991-6

10 9 8 7 6 5 4 3 2 1   20 19 18 17 16 15 14 13 12 11

CONTENTS

HOW TO **WOW** YOUR CHURCH GUESTS

With deep gratitude for my bride, best
friend, and life partner, Laura, and
our deep pride and only daughter, Liv—

you practice crazy, unconditional love
with me. You're the very best!

ACKNOWLEDGMENTS

t's impossible to acknowledge everyone who has inspired this short list of best practices. There are restaurant servers, cell phone representatives, and airline attendants whose names I never captured, but who set the customer service bar high for their companies (if only their companies had noticed). There are scores of local church volunteers and staff across the country who have shown me gracious hospitality. I can't name them all here. But here are a few of special note.

To my wife, Laura, and our daughter, Liv: thanks for your support, encouragement, and confidence. My transitions in ministry, leadership, and writing impact you, pulling you into my journey. I'm grateful you've joined that journey by choice.

To the hundreds of volunteer servants on multiple campuses called Granger Community Church: thank you for your impromptu acts of kindness, your heartfelt love for people, and your countless hours of time and energy leveraged to help people know they matter to God. You've created many of the practices here, and you continue to raise the bar with your excellence.

To contributors to this work: you represent hundreds of churches who have networked through training and conversations to collaboratively call the church to live out what it is intended to be—the embodiment of Jesus Christ, sharing his love unconditionally.

- Brian Marshall, pastor of connections, Foothills Community Church, Seneca, South Carolina
- Danny Franks, pastor of connections, Summit Church, Durham, North Carolina
- Katharine Sherwin, equipping director, Menlo Park Presbyterian Church, Menlo Park, California

- Katie Czapala, volunteer coordinator, TrueNorth Church, North Augusta, South Carolina

- Mike Feidler, pastor of missions, TrueNorth Church, North Augusta, South Carolina

- Stacey Windover, director of volunteers, West Bridge Church, Dallas, Georgia

To the team at Group Publishing: Amy Nappa, Bob D'Ambrosio, and Tim Willms, thank you for your trust and one more partnership in equipping and empowering the local church.

To my staff team at Granger Community Church: Mark Beeson, Tim Stevens, Rob Wegner, Jason Miller, DC Curry, Kem Meyer, Julie Sinies, Susan Chipman, Kathy Guy, Dawn Lovitt, Kim Volheim, Dian Brown, Vanessa Sanders, Amanda Harris, Don Reynolds, Liane Endres, and Shari Wolfgang—there's not a better group of people on the planet. Your towering gifts, your passion for Jesus, and your commitment to his agenda lift me and call me to be all he made me to be. I'm honored to serve alongside you.

What you hold in your hand started as a series of blog posts back in 2009. After nearly 50 best practice posts, a friend suggested, "You know you could bind these and make them available as a book, right?" (Thanks, Tim…and no, at the time I had no idea. I need my friends.) So, I've continued to make observations of my own experiences, listened to the experiences of others, and made careful notes. This little volume isn't exhaustive, but it's a pretty decent start at identifying best practices that will help you serve your guests with greater care and excellence.

Some phrases get thrown around with little to no explanation. Phrases like "a stitch in time saves nine" or "the cat's meow" or "the bee's knees." Huh? Other phrases are so overused, they've lost their once headline-making intensity. Phrases like "paradigm shift," "new economy," and "bandwidth" either redefined a previously understood word or with overuse minimized the critical nature of the topic being discussed.

"Best practice" runs the same risk. Maybe a brief explanation is helpful. BusinessDictionary.com provides the following definition of a "best practice:" _Methods_ and _techniques_ that have consistently shown _results_ superior than those achieved with other _means_, and which are used as _benchmarks_ to strive for.

Years ago Westin's "heavenly bed" set a best practice in the hotel industry for me. Jet Blue established best practices for in-air technology and entertainment. Disney has nailed so many best practices that both churches and the marketplace have learned from their guest services savvy.

Consider this book a start. Just 101 benchmarks that, if you embrace and practice even half of them, you'll exponentially lift the quality of your guest services in your local church or organization. Once you read the book, keep your eyes open. You'll create more. You and the teams you serve with have the potential to establish the list of best practices that will serve your culture and community uniquely.

BusinessDictionary.com concludes the definition for "best practice" this way: *There is, however, no practice that is best for everyone or in every situation, and no best practice remains best for very long as people keep on finding better ways of doing things.*

I dare you: keep finding better ways of doing what you do. Make this book obsolete. That's my hope.

Mark L. Waltz

Granger, Indiana

June 2011

#1 Don't Play Copycat

It's tempting. Pick up a book with that one inspiring chapter, and overhaul your small-group ministry. Attend a two-day conference on innovation, and scratch your entire weekend strategy and start over. Visit another church, take pictures, interview staff, go home… and resign. It's tempting.

Don't do it. Don't look at inspiration and assume the Holy Spirit is calling you to fire all your small-group leaders. Don't get hyped on innovation and torch the organ. Don't visit another church, become so convinced of what you're not, and quit.

Ministry isn't a rubber stamp. Your church isn't exactly like another. Your context isn't identical to someone else's. Don't try to copy everything that somehow seems "better." You'll never be Disney. You're not Willow Creek (unless you *are* Willow Creek). You're not Nordstrom. You can't be all things to all people.

It's tempting to think that because "it" worked well for them, it will work for us. But valet parking may not work in your context. The liability, the insurance restrictions, and your parking configuration may make it a really bad idea. Free coffee might drain your budget when you try to provide it for 400 or 4,000 guests. There may be another way to communicate value and infuse community into your environment. Rubber stamps work in kindergarten classrooms, high school print shops, and warehouses, but they rarely make a church or service organization better.

However, pay careful attention to best practices in hospitals, airports, shopping centers, websites, churches, amusement parks, theaters, gyms, airlines, and hotels. Not all the best practices you observe are universal, but many are. Still, you'll create many more by observing the inspiring individuals within your setting. You can't rubber-stamp success, but best practices that are repeated over and over become cultural norms that establish unique wins for you, your teams, and the people you serve.

Learn from the best, become better than you are, and teach someone else what you're learning. It's all we've ever done at Granger Community Church.

#2 | Pray

It's easy to think we've got this whole guest services thing locked up. We've read the books, studied great businesses, learned from other churches, stockpiled our own rich experiences. We've got this.

I get that God has wired a bunch of us for this. I understand that he works through us and through our gifted team members. But sometimes we soar along on our own, missing the fact that there's either something supernatural going on in these relational encounters—or there's not.

This is more than technique. More than a book of "best practices." We've been invited to God's agenda to redeem and recreate his creation. We're in on his movement to restore human life. This is his kingdom. We're mere citizens and stewards of his work.

I need my eyes constantly open to see what God is up to in my life and the lives of those around me. I need my ears alert to the faint whispers of his Spirit that help me be in the right place at the right time. I need my heart tuned to his agenda so the frustrations, details, and tasks don't become routine. I need my soul awakened to the present moment with the unique individuals in the moment, lest I merely perform a job— paid or unpaid.

I need to pray.

Are you praying?

WORST PRACTICE

Remember, this is your gig. Your agenda. Your church. Besides, if you take time to pray, you might not stay on task. Whatever you do, bluster through on your own wisdom and strength. Your agenda. Your church.

#3 | **Expect New People**

This really happened to me.

I walked into a restaurant with my family early in the lunch hour. Like, 11:00 a.m. On the dot. As in, I was the first customer of the day. Surveying the place, I saw…well, nothing. Lots of open tables. And still I was told, "Give me just a couple of minutes and we'll have a table for you." I could see at least 12,000 seating options. But I waited.

As I sat down I intuitively wiped bread crumbs from the table onto the floor and thought, "This doesn't make sense. There's no way there have been other customers in here for lunch already." Of course, the mess had to have been left over from the night before. We then learned that the coffee and tea were still brewing. I would have been okay if the posted opening time was 11:16 a.m. If they needed a few more minutes to prepare the place, I could have waited and shown up then.

Bottom line? This staff wasn't ready for us. They weren't really expecting customers—not this early, anyway.

How about your church? Is it apparent that you're expecting new people? Do first-arriving guests catch you by surprise? Here are some simple ways to communicate, "We've been expecting you!"

- A core of people who know church isn't all about them, but about others, so they…
  - give up their front parking spaces
  - move to the center of the row, leaving the aisle seats open
  - greet people around them—even when they're not "on" as an usher or greeter
- Smiling parking attendants in the parking lot
- Cordial greeters at entry doors and accommodating ushers throughout the building
- Signage that points to "new family children's area" or "guest services"
- A verbal welcome from the front of the room that includes new guests (without embarrassing them)

- A program/bulletin that speaks to new people, using "normal" language
- Visible, accessible "on-ramps" that help new people connect and grow

When your guests show up, will they think, "Wow! They acted like they were expecting me and they were happy about it!" Or will they feel as if they've crashed a party they weren't invited to attend?

How are you planning for, and expecting, new guests at your church?

#4 | Make Room

Our senior pastor, Mark Beeson, says often, "New people can really be a headache for churched people. New people expect a parking space, a place to sit, and a place for their kids. And they don't know that *you* already have a choice parking space, a favorite seat, and a place for your kids." When a church is intentional about reaching new people who don't know they matter to God, new people *will* show up. And they *will* take your parking spot, and they *will* sit in your seat, and they *will* crowd your children's space.

Are you okay with that?

The reality is many churches are not. By churches, of course, I mean people—'cause the church is people.

I've visited churches that appear to be thoughtful about new guests by providing designated parking for guests. But there are only three spaces reserved! Really? You expected three guests? That's it? I've heard horror stories of church members standing in an aisle telling a guest, "That's my seat." Argggh...

Are you making room for new guests? Are you communicating that you expect them?

What about:

- asking your volunteers, staff, and members to park in the parking spaces farthest from the building, leaving the front spaces for your newer guests?

- designated parking for guests—and making sure it's adequate for the guests you're expecting?

- using ushers to seat guests, providing them choice seats without regard for "owned" seats?

- putting traffic teams in the parking lot whose job it is to not only direct traffic, but provide a warm welcome before guests and members reach the building?

What are you doing to make room for new people?

When I visit a city other than my own, I often wander into a local mall to pick up a memento for my wife or daughter. If I know the kind of store I want to find—clothing store, music store, novelty store—I look first for the mall directory.

I have a clear vision. I know what I'm looking for. I've already pictured the kind of thing I want to carry out of the mall when I leave. So, I look for the store most likely to sell that product. But I look for a secondary item on the mall directory. I look for the X or the arrow that defines, "You Are Here." I could wander the mall and eventually find the store in my vision. But I will find it more efficiently and effectively if I first identify where I am.

And even though I want to be in that store, I'm not. I'm right here where the X says I am. This is where I have to start. Then, and only then, can I chart a path that will get me from veracity (what is real) to my vision (where I want to be).

At Granger, we decided a long time ago to simply meet people where they are. Our mission is "helping people take their next step toward Christ…together." Our mission motivates us to create a safe and welcoming environment for our guests. Our mission drives us to meet people where they are, not where we wish they were.

If we expect to help people take their next step, they can only take it from where they are. They can't be anywhere but there. If we're going to help them take their next step, we'll have to meet them there—right where the X says they are.

WORST PRACTICE

Don't let people drag you down to their level. If people want to belong to your church, they'll need to learn the language, clean up their lives, and carry a Bible. They did come to church, after all.

#6 | **Understand Base Fears**

Understand that people are fearful.
New guests fear the unknown. Will
I have to speak? Will they ask for my
money? Will they expect me to sing?
How will I know when to sit, stand,
kneel, cross myself, speak, or cry? What
if I fall asleep and snore? People show
up in our churches with several of
these fears.

If we really get that they're afraid,
we'll likely treat them differently,
thoughtfully.

Go ahead. Think about it.

How would you interact with
someone who is actually fearful about
walking into your church? How would
you want your own fears addressed?

#7 | Prepare Your Mind

It was scary the first time I experienced it. Then it just got weirder to me when it happened again. And then again. It's happened to you, too. You're driving a routine route to work or along a familiar stretch of road. Minutes pass. Miles accumulate. Suddenly you arrive at your destination and realize that you have no memory of the past several, maybe many, miles and minutes. You can't recall stoplights, traffic, or landmarks you've driven past. It's weird. Even scary.

We shift into autopilot all too easily. And it's not limited to our driving.

How easy is it to rush into a guest service opportunity from home, work, or even the church office...on autopilot? You've done it so many times, you've stopped thinking about it. You're ticking through your unfinished task list; you're processing what you still need to do after you serve guests; you give little thought to what's about to happen.

Practice these three simple steps to prepare your mind to serve people:

1. STOP: Breathe. You'll strip emotional gears trying to move from one focus to the next. Ultimately, you'll not be fully present. You'll move into the present with one foot in your unfinished task list and another in the moment just ahead. Slow down.

2. PRAY: Ask God to help you engage. Think about where you're headed. Why what you're about to do even matters. Get perspective on his agenda.

3. FOCUS: Be present. Live in the moment. Make eye contact with everyone you engage. Be ready, usable, and open.

Prepare your mind. People know when your body is present but your mind is in another zip code.

#8　Go Fishing

I'm a bit of an introvert. Ironic, huh? The connecting guy is shy. Kinda. When I'm not in my own environment (i.e., my home, my church, my friends), I feel pretty safe up against the wall by myself. However, when I'm in my passion area—in my environment—I try to meet new people.

Jason Hester, executive pastor of ministries at Pinelake Church in Brandon, Mississippi, calls it "fishing." He patrols the hallways, looking for people who look "lost." When he identifies them, he tries to "catch them," welcome them, and help them feel at home.

It's tempting for most of us to gravitate toward our friends—introvert or extrovert. We enjoy the community and the safety of talking with people we know. But on the weekends at your church, it's not just about you. It's about others. Others who don't have a friend to gravitate toward…not yet, anyway.

Look around. Go fishing.

#9 | Ask for Feedback

It's amazing how well we think we're doing when our only evaluation is our own. It's also easy to hear feedback from our "churched" crowd and think we're delivering great guest service. But remember, churched people have very different expectations than your newest guest who is not a regular church-goer. Getting feedback from our newest guests risks that we'll have to work through:

- misperceptions about our values
- language barriers because guests don't know "insider" church/Bible talk
- expectations that we haven't thought about

However, being intentional about getting feedback from your guests will...

- help you communicate real value to people right where they are
- cause you to focus on base-level service like the environment that's created at your church and how guests are followed up on
- allow you to be consistent in your training with your team members

There are a number of ways to get this feedback. And by feedback, I mean about anything and everything: your parking lot, your campus/property, your building, restrooms, kids' space, warmth/friendliness, café/hospitality, your service, and your print pieces. Here are just a few ways to ask for input:

- Ask for feedback on your comment/prayer card in your weekend program/bulletin.

    ➤ *We've done this every week for years. It's a weekly, instant survey.*

- Send a letter asking for a brief survey to be completed.

    ➤ *My friend Danny Franks, pastor of connections and campus pastor at The Summit Church in Durham, NC sends a letter to every new guest with a postage-paid survey card. He provides space for four responses:*

- This is what I noticed first…
- This is what I liked best…
- This is what I liked least…
- This is what I am most looking for in a church…

● Form a focus group of people who are no more than six months new to your church.

> *They're new enough to have not forgotten their first experience, but they've been around long enough to give you honest feedback.*

● Hire or bring in your own "secret shoppers" who score everything related to the guest experience at your church.

WORST
PRACTICE

Don't seek feedback. Guests don't understand your values, intentions, or theology. Asking them for feedback on your church experience is like a car manufacturer asking a driver for feedback on a car. What does a driver know?

> *We've used GuestReflections.com services. They are a "secret shopper" service for churches. They're thorough, very thorough (as in ten pages of reporting from the parking lot to children's ministry to signage to the service itself…); they miss nothing.*

> *We've brought our own mystery shoppers in on more than one occasion. We don't pay them. We do give them a small amount of cash to use in our bookstore and/or cafe, so they can experience the service in those venues and give us a first-hand evaluation.*

> *When we bring in any mystery shopper, we prioritize using those who do not regularly attend church. They tend to offer more honest reflections. Besides, we'd rather hear from an unchurched focus audience. Churched folks have different expectations than new, non-churchgoing guests.*

> *We haven't scored 100% from any of our mystery shopper experiences. The point is not to score, frame, and celebrate the A+; the point is to get honest feedback so you can improve your service to your guests.*

Get feedback. Then act on it to improve the way you communicate that people matter to God... and to you.

#10 | Never Assume

Never assume. This happens all the time. You step up to a salesclerk in a store; they may assume you want help with the product line they represent. Nope. All you want is directions to the restroom. It takes you awhile to wade through the sales pitch they assume you want to hear, but finally you ask, "Where's the restroom?"

And it happens in churches, too. Guests may stop an usher and announce that they are new to your church. The temptation from the well-intended team member may be to download everything he or she thinks a new person may want to know.

- *We have 19 services this weekend, including contemporary, jazz, gospel, and hip-hop.*

- *This is our statement of beliefs. The 47 pages may be a bit much to read right now, so let me point out the biggies.*

- *Oh look, you have kids. Our children's center was built just 4 years ago and covers 110,000 square feet. Here's a news article that our local paper ran on opening weekend.*

- *Our pastor has been here since 1953. He's retiring—finally—we were afraid we were going to have to carry him out!*

You get the point.

Again, maybe all that the guest wanted was directions to the service... or the restroom.

When a guest asks a question, use questions in return to fully understand what's being asked. Assume nothing.

There's an old saying that says when you assume, you make an... never mind.

#11 Listen to Complaints

It happens. You've heard them. People make comments that are less than complimentary, even disparaging. You don't want to listen. You want to turn it off. You want to find some "yes" people and tune them in. But what you must do is listen.

- If one person is making the observation (that'd be the complaint), 10 more people may be thinking the same thing. They just didn't have the courage to say so. You must listen.

- The person may not understand your values, methods, or language, but if you'll listen, you may learn what people are actually hearing—even if you don't intend to communicate it. You can learn.

- There's usually at least a grain of truth—even if the complaint is riddled with emotion and misinformed statements. Find the truth.

- A primary concern (in addition to your faithfulness to the message of Jesus) should be how people are hearing and experiencing your message—from the parking lot to the spoken message, from the care expressed in your systems to the personal connection points. Perception matters.

- Often people who share legitimate concerns are people who can help bring solutions to your systems and organization. Enlist their help.

One more thought—if you're the one making a complaint, have the courage to use your name. When you do, conversation can be constructive and helpful. To both parties. When you don't, you're cowardly and your comment is likely to be taken that way. Own it, respectfully. Open dialogue focused on mutual outcomes can reveal blind spots and pathways to improvement.

Again, if you're positioned to hear complaints, shut up already and listen.

WORST PRACTICE

People are always bellyaching about how they weren't satisfied. You don't have time to listen to that. People need to grow up. Ignore them.

#12 | Names = Value

You won't remember everyone's name, but you should try. Get over the false expectation that you're going to always remember names. When you forget, just be honest. You forgot. Or you have no idea if you've met before. Just admit it: I don't remember.

If yours is a familiar face around your church, lots of people will remember and call you by name. And there's a fair chance you won't always remember theirs. People are forgiving. Accept it. And as you do, practice something that helps you remember their name. Repeat it. Say it again at the end of the conversation. Play name association with someone they remind you of. Write it down as soon as you walk away. Ask for a spelling (Kathy—with a "k" or a "c"; don't use this technique if the name is "Bob").

Names matter because people matter.

#13 | Read Body Language

It's really simpler than you think. Not everyone wants to shake hands. Churched people want handshakes (unless there's a swine flu scare, then no one wants a handshake); people new to your church may only want a courteous "hello." Read the body language of your guests to determine an appropriate greeting.

- Both hands are buried deeply in his pockets. He doesn't want to shake your hand.

- A parent is holding tightly to their kids' hands. Don't offer a handshake.

- Her eyes are focused on the carpet. She doesn't want to make eye contact. Probably not going to shake her hand. You may not even get the opportunity to speak as she passes.

- He's answering as briefly as possible while glancing at his watch every three seconds. He's not into your conversation. Don't trap him; let him go on his way.

- He stepped into the lobby and stopped for two seconds as he surveyed the space cautiously. He's likely new. Approach him with a personal introduction and a handshake.

- She's reading the weekend program (or bulletin) word for word. She's new. No one in your church reads it thoroughly. Opportunity to connect.

- He's standing alone in the hallway. Good chance he's waiting for his lady who's in the restroom. He hates this wait. He feels conspicuous. Eliminate the mystery: "Will someone try to talk to me?" Put him out of his misery. Introduce yourself.

Make instant assessments. If your guest is communicating, "Leave me alone," listen. Otherwise, extend a personal welcome.

#14 | Think One Chance

I remember a season when I experienced a fair amount of frustration with my cable company. In one week, three of four conversations with different reps left me feeling like I had done something wrong. I felt chided, even scolded a couple of times. I would have chucked the whole deal with them and gone to another provider, but I'm in an older neighborhood and...well, I feel stuck with my provider. So I negotiated and made the arrangement livable.

I'm really not that hard to get along with, honest. But, like you, there's something in me that knows I have personal value. And when we experience "customer service" that isn't "customer care," we feel devalued. Great service is about value.

You could eat a meal in a restaurant where the food is excellent. I mean the best you've ever eaten. But if the service is poor—slow, impersonal, or indifferent—you'll likely be so distracted by the lack of service that it will be all you talk about throughout the meal. And there's a fair chance you'll miss just how superb the meal is.

That's why we'll switch cable companies (if it's possible), avoid a fee-gouging airline, or stop going to a restaurant that can't seem to get our steak cooked as requested. We're not snobs. We just know that personal value can be communicated effectively, so we go to places, businesses, and providers where that's our consistent experience.

Your guests in your church do the same thing. Every weekend.

They assess, involuntarily, the sense of personal value they experience. It could be the best message your pastor has ever preached. You could have the most inspiring media and impactful music. But if your guests didn't feel welcomed, and they found the restroom dirty, the parking lot difficult to navigate, or the children's room crowded, they may sit in your service and completely miss the message that they matter to God.

They may choose, in one visit, to not return simply because they didn't experience personal value. Call it guest services, call it customer care, call it ministry. The label doesn't matter. Your people will experience personal value—or not. And they'll make decisions about returning to your church based on it.

You may only get one chance.

What are you doing to make that one weekend for that one guest be an experience of personal value? Will people be distracted by the lack of care or embraced by the excellence of it? Will they leave and not return or come back to experience the love of Christ through his people?

Think "one chance."

WORST PRACTICE

Don't get stressed out about how someone may or may not respond to the service. If they come back, God wanted them there. If not, wipe your feet and be done. Next.

#15 | Create On-Ramps

Create a great welcome, but don't stop there. Create an engaging experience that leads to a next step. While you want your guests to feel "at home" in their visit to your church, it's not enough for them to merely feel good about what's happening right now.

Inside that first experience, what are they called to in the future? What's next for them? What are the options?

- Why would they want to return?
- Why would they decide to attend a class?
- For what reason would they choose to participate in a group?
- What's the motivation to join a community service?

Paint clear, visible on-ramps that create the opportunity for movement.

#16 | Give 'Em Something to Talk About

They will talk. Your guests will tell their friends about your church. What if they say they were treated unkindly, if they were treated at all? What if they tell a friend they'll never go back? What if they say they didn't really connect with the service or message at all?

Unless you give them something to talk about, you have little idea what your guests will tell others about your church. Determine in advance what you'd like guests to tell someone else, and then go about building teams, creating environments, and developing processes that do just that.

You want your guests talking about how personable your greeters are? Build your team with personable, gregarious people. You want your guests to tell others that they're going back next week? Create ways to communicate value and relevance.

Go ahead. Give 'em something to talk about.

#17 | Surprise Your Guests

I'm not talking about jumping out from behind trash cans and scaring your guests. That'd be a surprise, but no. And I'm not thinking about blowing your budget to lavish your guests with extravagant gifts that they'll leave in your trash can or the floorboard of their car.

Think simple. Think functional. Think

- umbrella escorts in inclement weather
- hand sanitizer dispensers around your building
- chairs/lounge area in the women's restroom
- clean everything…then keep it clean
- follow-up when guests request help
- mouthwash, lotion, mints in the restrooms
- soft seating in common areas
- remember their name
- pay attention to their kids
- listen to them
- take them home-baked bread on Sunday afternoon
- send a thank-you note
- use language they understand
- _____ (fill in the blank)

The point isn't to merely surprise your guests for the sake of surprise. Rather, the carefully planned surprise communicates care and value.

What is it that your guests are *not* expecting?

Do that.

WORST PRACTICE

Be boring. Look bored. Act bored. Interact as little as possible. Validate what people already think of church: boring.

#18 | Host a Meet-n-Greet

People want to know the pastor. There are too many reasons to list them all here. But for starters, people think of the pastor they hear teaching every weekend as their shepherd, their caregiver. They want to be known. They want to feel personally cared for.

Depending on the size of your church, you may have great systems and strategies for personal care that include other pastors, directors, and teams of volunteers. However, tremendous value is communicated to guests when they are able to get directly to staff, including the senior/teaching pastor.

At Granger we host a periodic "Meet-n-Greet," inviting new guests to meet our senior pastor. As they wait to say hello, a number of other staff and spouses greet the line of people. During those conversations, we're able to hear enough of the guests' stories to offer next steps for their journey toward Jesus at Granger.

People experience personal value because suddenly their assumption that "this church is too big to meet the pastor" is blown away. Additionally, because they've stepped out of the "crowd" of the weekend service and taken a step to be known, the majority take a next step almost immediately.

I first experienced this "meet the pastor" at Mosaic, a church in Los Angeles, CA, where lead pastor Erwin McManus hosts a "10-Minute Party" after the weekend service. His time there is focused specifically on meeting and communicating personal value to new guests.

At Central Baptist in Jonesboro, Arkansas, Pastor Archie Mason and his wife, Angie, meet guests every weekend after each of their three services. They simply hang out near their Connection Café to meet, mingle, and encourage. In almost every interaction they're able to point guests to a specific next step. The greeting doesn't stop there—Archie and Angie help people engage life in the church body.

Host an opportunity for people to meet your pastor. Your pastor may not remember every name, but the intentional touch will communicate the care people desire to experience and the connection you want to provide.

#19 Remember the Introverts

Consider the typical profile of top-notch guest services personnel:

- Extroverted
- Bubbly
- Smiling
- Enthusiastic
- First to engage others

And those are tremendous qualities in people who serve the "public." Unfortunately, many organizations—businesses and churches—assume those being greeted are as extroverted as the extroverts who serve them. It just isn't so.

Truth is, I'm somewhat of an introvert. In my own space, in my own passion area, in my ministry focus—I look very much like an extrovert. Talkative, willing to engage people I don't already know, a real mix-it-up kind of guy. Otherwise, on someone else's turf, outside my own realm, I'm less talkative and a bit withdrawn.

So when I drive onto someone else's church campus and see signs directing me to "first-time visitor parking," I intentionally turn the other direction. Any other direction. Here's what I accurately expect: in that "special" lot, I'll be greeted by over-enthusiastic parking attendants who know I'm "new;" I'll encounter the same zeal by the specially selected greeters who'll treat me like royalty, offering everything from an escort to a guest reception area to a full body massage (well, maybe not the massage…although I might take them up on that one).

I avoid the spotlight.

When I did this at a church in central Texas, my chosen parking lot was near an entrance that took me into the children's area where there were no greeters. This church hadn't considered introverts in their guest services plan.

I know a lady in our church who held tightly to the hands of her twin girls as she entered our church each week—not because she feared she'd lose them, but because she wanted to avoid shaking the hand of any of our people.

I've watched people enter our building with their eyes to the ground and their hands deeply in their pockets. I don't know if they were mad or sad; they may have been quite glad. But they wanted to protect their space...their personal, introverted space.

Train the extroverts! Put engaging people on your front line! But train them to relate to the introverts, too.

#20 | Don't Embarrass

Your intentions are good: you want to recognize every new guest. You don't want them to feel left out or ignored. Awesome! Just exercise some caution and don't embarrass them in the process.

I have a friend who moved to the West from our church years ago. The following is her story from one church she visited shortly after her move:

"At the end of the service, the pastor asked all the members and regular attendees to stand. So of course I remained seated. Then he announced, 'Let's welcome our visitors.' Everyone standing surrounded the few now-stunned visitors—and they broke into a song of welcome! I was mortified. It was my one and only visit to that church."

WORST PRACTICE

Do anything you can to draw attention to your guests. Capture their names prior to the service so the pastor can work their names into illustrations in his message. Better yet, take their pictures and project them on the big screen. They'll feel so included!

She would have taken a rose sticker (remember those?) to wear. She would have gladly received a welcome packet. Anything but a song and a spotlight.

Make your guests feel welcome. Be warm and personable. Just don't embarrass them in the process.

#21 | **Introductions Are Personal**

My wife, Laura, had invited her friend Karen to join her for a weekend service numerous times. Ultimately, Karen agreed to meet her at Granger one Sunday morning for service. Laura was serving at our guest services center that weekend, so she was easy for Karen to find. Laura was thrilled!

Laura dismissed herself from the kiosk and immediately began to introduce Karen to a number of her other friends. That morning she introduced Karen to three or four people, anticipating that when Karen returned (she was pretty confident Karen would love her experience and want to come back), the odds were a little higher that she might recognize someone she knew. Granted, a small handful of people among hundreds weren't fantastic odds, but a few is better than one.

Karen did in fact return the next week. And on that Sunday, Laura introduced Karen to several more friends. On the third week she did the same. In her first month at Granger, Karen had met nearly a dozen new people. Karen was beginning to feel like this was her church, not merely her friend Laura's church.

Laura's introductions communicated value in a number of ways:

- When people hear their name in any positive sense, it conveys personal value. Karen was on a first-name basis with a dozen people in under a month.
- Laura's Granger friends heard, "There's room for more in our circle of friendships." Their sense of inclusion was encouraged.
- Laura communicated to her friends that they were important enough to her to have them meet another friend. Value was communicated to everyone in that four-week series of introductions.

Karen now comes and goes at Granger on her own. She is known by a growing number of people who know her name. Introductions are personal.

#22 | Don't Be Too Friendly

About four years into my staff role at Granger, I was surprised to read several individual comments from guests attending our weekend service:

"Too friendly."

I scoffed as I read the cards. "Too friendly?" I thought. "Fine. Go somewhere else. There are plenty of rigid, staunch, cold, unfriendly churches around. We're working hard at this!"

Shortly after these comments, we invited some "secret shoppers" from our community to give us some honest feedback about their experience at our church. I was appalled. *"Too friendly."*

This was too honest to be coincidental. I had to put my big boy pants on and stop being so defensive. Our team sat down to evaluate how someone could possibly think we were too friendly. With an honest audit, it didn't take long to see their point.

We had a team of people in the parking lot, directing, welcoming, yelling, "Welcome! Glad you're here!" There were greeters on the curb, shaking hands, saying the same thing. We had more greeters positioned at the entry doors of the building. Same thing. Our "campus guides"—teams of people looking to engage new guests and help them find their way around the campus—positioned themselves across the width of our atrium, allowing no one to pass without a formal greeting. At the auditorium—or worship center—doors with more greeters, passing out service programs with a warm smile and "welcome!" Inside, our ushers were greeting and offering to help the same guests find a seat.

We concluded: *"Okay. Maybe it's possible. Perhaps there's a chance someone might think we're too friendly."*

Ya think?!

So we relaxed. We didn't stop greeting guests. We didn't pull our traffic team out of the parking lot. But we did pull back on the handshakes. We shifted our focus to reading the body language of our guests. We let them "tell us" how they wanted to be greeted. We agreed that being authentically caring as a people would minimize the chance that someone would see us as "too friendly"

#23 Say "No" Creatively

I hate hearing "no." Hate it.

- In a retail store: Do you have this pair of pants in a 31x32?
  - ➤ "No. I'm sorry."

- At a hotel: Can I get free Wi-Fi in my room?
  - ➤ "No. We just have hard-wire data lines."

- In a theater: Can you adjust the temperature?
  - ➤ "No. That's not my job."

- On the phone: May I speak to your manager?
  - ➤ "No. He'd tell you the same thing I just told you."

- At a local church: Do you offer childcare for your adult classes?
  - ➤ "No. You'll have to arrange your own childcare."

I hate hearing "no."

In fact, I believe each of the above questions can be answered differently, resulting in a positive experience for the customer or guest:

- In a retail store: Do you have this pair of pants in a 31x32?
  - ➤ "Let's see what I have." or "Yes, I can order that for you."

- At a hotel: Can I get free Wi-Fi in my room?
  - ➤ "I have a complimentary data line for your room. You may access our free wi-fi in the lobby and restaurant. If you choose either of those, please enjoy a complimentary drink as you do."

- In a theater: Can you adjust the temperature?
  - ➤ "I can't guarantee that it'll be satisfactory in the next few minutes, but I'll do what I can to make it more comfortable. Thank you for your feedback."

- On the phone: May I speak to your manager?
  - ➤ "Of course. I'm sorry I was not able to adequately resolve this for you. Please hold."

- At a local church: Do you offer childcare for your adult classes?
  - "At present we're able to open as many rooms for children as we have volunteers to staff them. We value the safety and care of your children, so we will open rooms as we have an adequate number of leaders."

Sometimes the answer is "no." But there's almost always another way to say "no" other than "no." This is not about "spin" or mere creative language. It is about communicating care and understanding. It is about the golden rule.

You remember that one, don't you?

WORST PRACTICE

Sometimes the answer is just "no." People have been trained that the "customer is always right." Wrong. When you need to say "no," say "no." "No— the temperature is set." "No—you may not take your drink into the worship center." "No—the volume cannot be turned up." No is no.

#24 Invite Them Back

Ever go on a first date that left you wondering if there'd be a second opportunity? Maybe the end of the evening was awkward at best because there was no "I'll call you" or "I had a nice time. Can I see you again?" So you watched your phone for a text or an e-mail, but it never chimed, dinged, or rang.

It's pretty simple. Invite your guests back. Say it from the platform. Make the invitation personally with an exit greeting. Extend your welcome.

Don't leave your guests feeling like a jilted date waiting by the phone to see if there'll be a request for a second date.

#25 | Say "Thank You"

Gratitude is too easily lost in a "me first" society bent toward a sense of personal entitlement. Even in the church it's easy to blow off expressions of gratitude, thinking everything our people are doing should be for God anyway. While that's the motivation we're praying for, it doesn't excuse any of us from being grateful humans, reflecting and expressing personal value to others.

Here's a quick list of "thanks" that are worth expressing to your people—guests, members, and volunteers:

- Open your service with "grateful you've decided to be here today." People have options. Lots of options. They chose to come to church.

- Express thanks for the contribution people make in giving and volunteering—from the platform in the service.

- Thank people personally for attending the service—we call it "exit greeting."

- Thank your volunteers with public parties/gatherings.

- Tell your volunteers personally how much you value their time, expertise, willingness, and unique contribution.

- Send a letter, make a phone call—thank your first-time guests for joining you for service. Remember, they had options.

When you express thanks, you honor people by recognizing the choice they've exercised to give time, expend resources, make sacrifices, and take next steps in their spiritual journey. Respect people. Value them. Say "thank you."

WORST PRACTICE

Don't thank your guests. Your guests have done you no favors by showing up at your church. Remember—they've taken prime seats, stolen your parking space, and will require you to give more, 'cause they won't.

#26 Don't Forget the Kids

It's really this simple: Show appropriate attention to my child, and I'll know you like me. Love my child, love me. Value my child, value me.

So when greeting guests, pay attention to their children. Don't assume all the value they need has been expressed in your children's ministry area. High five, get on their level, talk with children. I guarantee you: your adult guests will be impressed! And their children will feel valued.

#27 Give 'Em a D.A.M. Bag

No. Don't swear at or about your guests. Keep reading.

Families arrive late for our services. It happens. Every week. No kidding. If families arrive too late in the service, our children's rooms are closed. We provide a family-friendly alternative in our connection café where our guests can take in the service via large-screen monitors—and enjoy a beverage.

Our volunteer guest relations team noticed over several weeks that as accommodating as we were, the children were often bored after their cookie was gone. So Deb had an idea: put together a simple kid's bag with coloring activities, crayons, information on children's ministries (including service times), and a café coupon. She e-mailed the idea, and the inner-office e-mail chain took off.

Wanting to keep the idea credited to the appropriate volunteer, her initials were tied to the bag: the D.A.M.—Deborah A. Miller—bags.

Here's the point: cultivate a culture where volunteers own the ministry. And then give them credit when they lead out and create initiatives that serve your guests well.

Oh, and pay attention to opportunities to add value to your guests. Even late-arriving guests.

WORST PRACTICE

You cannot reward or tolerate late-comers. You must enforce punctuality. Provide late-arriving guests with a printed piece with bolded service times, asking them to please be courteous to other guests and respectful of God by being early next week.

#28 Identify the Flashers

Danny Franks and his teams at Summit Church in Durham, North Carolina, have provided specially reserved guest parking near the main doors of their church building and adjacent to their first-time guest tent (they can do that kind of outdoorsy thing in the South). Danny says a best practice at the Summit is "turn on your flashers."

At each of their four campuses, the entry points have huge signs on the side of the road that ask first-time guests to turn on their hazard lights. Doing so allows their parking attendants to direct them to their guest parking.

So what about introverts? Don't worry. They'll likely ignore the "flasher" instructions. Just be certain to create a warm and safe reception for them as well. You still want to communicate personal value.

For everyone else, it's a practice that values new people by giving them red carpet treatment. They know not everyone is getting this spotlight. And their members and regular attendees know not everyone is getting this privileged parking. It reminds them that other people matter, that new people are honored guests.

That deserves some blinking lights.

#29 One Thing, Only One

People have questions. Lots of questions. So we work hard to make sure our campus guides and guest relations teams have all the info: classes, groups, children's offerings, vision, values. We want to resource them well to answer guests' questions.

However, if your teams are spilling out all they know to every new person, someone should crimp the fire hose! Katharine Sherwin, equipping director at Menlo Park Presbyterian Church in Menlo Park, California, trains her teams to quickly identify the ONE thing the guest most needs now. If they're only asking for directions to the restroom, help them find it. If the guest needs to know where the adult Bible class is meeting, guide them. If they want information about meeting others at the church, provide information about gatherings and venues where that can happen.

Don't overwhelm them with what you know. Listen. Ask questions. Care enough to be curious about their real interest. Then point to the ONE thing that best addresses their interest or need.

One thing, only one.

#30 Don't Give People the Finger

This is great advice, but it's probably not what you're thinking. This is a best practice Doug Dreeson, pastor of mission at Manassas Assembly of God, Manassas, Virginia, teaches his teams. And no, it's not about avoiding flipping the bird at guests (regardless of how they may gesture in the parking lot).

Simply: Never point directions for a guest. Always escort. Always.

Stop what you're doing and respond to the guest's request for directions to the restroom, the auditorium, the four-year-old room. Don't point: "See that blue sign? Just past the sign turn left down the hallway. Go all the way to the end, make a right at the double doors. Just past the double doors, you'll see a bright orange tent. That's not it. Keep going. At the second orange tent, make a right. Go down the stairs, first door on your left. Can't miss it." Right. Try that, you might get the finger.

Never point. Always escort. Always.

Remember Something; Remember Anything

Harold remembers. Harold was born in 1936 and has been part of Granger Community Church since 1998. He's no spring chicken, but don't tell him that. Harold not only remembers names, but he almost always "remembers" and brings up an event, a relative, a conversation with the person he's talking with. And he'll often bring another bystander into the conversation to celebrate the memory. Of course, he's not celebrating the memory as much as he's honoring the person he's engaging.

- I remember that cake you baked.

- Your dad loves you so much.

- You've got the voice of an angel.

When Harold remembers more than a name, the person he's connecting with hears, "I value you. I know you. I haven't forgotten you. You matter."

There may be one more key to Harold's remembering. Harold is a grateful man. Joy and thanks characterize his life lens. That helps him focus on others as part of a lifestyle, not just a role.

I want to be like Harold when I grow up.

#32 Follow-Up

Confession: Follow-up is something I have to work at—a lot. It doesn't come easily. I like moving on to something new. I like a new project, a new focus, a new step. Then I move on.

Consider this book. I began working on it months and months before it was finished. Then something else came along. Another phone call came in. I met another friend. Life happened, and it keeps happening. The book was put on hold. Friendly accountability and deadlines proved necessary in the follow-through.

At any point in time, whatever is happening "right now" is the most important thing happening in my world. Following up is challenging. It requires discipline.

But follow-up is about care. Care is communicated when I...

- follow-up on someone whose wife died a month ago
- return a call to a guest whose question wasn't answered over the weekend
- connect with a woman whose husband had a medical emergency during a service
- remember to ask a team member about her job interview
- call a guest by name after the service is over—one hour after I first met him
- respond to an e-mail
- finish a book

How about you? What's in place to help you remember? To follow-up? What's in place to make sure your volunteers and staff team do the same? What's still sitting on your desk? Who is it you need to call? Who would benefit from a quick note?

Set the book down a minute, maybe two. Pick up the phone, a pen, a keyboard. Follow up.

People really do matter.

#33 Get Unstuck

Even "wow" can get stale. Of course, then it's not "wow" anymore. Don't miss this: what's "wow" today will fade. What's high value today can become the expected.

You will lose momentum. You will get stuck. Maybe you are stuck. Get unstuck.

- Take the lid off (you might have to pry hard). Knock the sides off the box (go crazy, pound hard).
- Invite new ideas (from anyone, everyone).
- Don't block (with budget constraints, staff cutbacks, or church policy).
- Honestly consider all new ideas.
- Think simple, too. Sometimes simple is the big "wow."
- Where could you empower your teams to create "moments" in the moment?
- Would a different volunteer schedule serve guests better?
- Would a different leadership team serve team members better?
- How can you say "Thanks, we're glad you're here" to guests in ways you've not said it before?
- Experiment. Try it once.
- Stop doing something you've always done. See what happens.
- Budget service.
- Remember, think simple.

Don't stop the process until you see your teams owning the process of becoming "unstuck." Stay at it until you see positive impact on your environment and guests. Press against the norm until you can look over your shoulder and identify new best practices that have increased your impact.

WORST PRACTICE

Ruts are good. They're familiar, comfortable, and cozy. Don't merely be stuck; wallow in the mud of your never-changing methods. Let the weeds of irrelevance and old tradition choke the life out of your ministry.

#34 Remove Barriers

For years at Granger, our guest relations center was just that—a center. It was a room unto itself. The oversized transaction counter served as walls. The volunteer staff was protectively barricaded behind the desk, surrounded on all sides, keeping a safe distance from inquiring guests. I'll not try to support nor defend that decade-old decision.

We've replaced that fortress of a "welcome center" with small, free-standing 3-foot tables designed so volunteers cannot "hide" or retreat. While that was never their goal, the large desk served as a barrier, preventing guests from connecting relationally with the non-paid staff who really wanted to be helpful.

Look around. What could be a barrier to connecting? Is it the glass wall at the office desk? The forbidding welcome center? Signage on doors that reject "normal" people?

Remove the barriers. Even the sacred ones.

#35 | Hang a Sign

Self-disclosure #1: Pretty much any building I enter—restaurant, airport, mall, church, museum, store, your house—I'm looking for a restroom eventually. There aren't too many homes with signage for bathrooms, but I generally know the host, so I can ask.

When a new guest comes to your church, they're most likely to look for one of three things (maybe all three):

- restroom
- children's center
- auditorium or worship center

Self-disclosure #2: When we opened our new auditorium at our Granger site, we were strategic and careful about where signage was placed and just what it communicated. However, five years later I toured our building with my guest services coaches, and we made some disappointing discoveries. Some signage used a font that was too small to read without standing still. (People generally read directional signage on the move. Think airport.) Some signage was added much later, and secondary bulkheads hid the newer signage. Other signage used our in-house language that was not all that helpful to our guests.

So when hanging signage, ask:

- What are guests really looking for? Is a sign with an arrow to the recycle bin really all that helpful or necessary?
- If this sign were hanging in an airport, would guests see it as they rushed to catch a plane? If not, make the sign bigger. (If your church is smaller, think smaller airport...but think about people reading signage as they move.)
- Will people understand what "Kidutopia" means? Or would it be better to simply say "Kids' Center"?

Hang a sign. And hang it effectively.

#36 | Transform the Space

Mike Fiedler, missions pastor with TrueNorth Church in North Augusta, South Carolina, has been a key player since that church started in late summer 2004. Since that time, this church has met weekly in a high school. Their two additional sites also meet in rented space. Mike understands the need to transform space.

Mike says you must help people forget they're in a gym, movie theater, or cafeteria. Use pipe and drape, creative graphics, lighting, and seating to help people experience God without distractions.

It's critical to create physical environments that foster the experience you've planned. Do you want everyone focused on the message at the front of the room? Forward-facing rows of chairs will help. Do you want lots of conversation among those attending? Tables with a limited number of chairs will encourage talking.

Space can be too large, too small, too dark, too light, too loud, too quiet. Transform the space with your end goal in mind. I'll bet your end goal is to help people see and hear Jesus clearly. Use your space to accomplish just that.

WORST PRACTICE

Just focus on the message of Jesus. Don't get sidelined trying to fix the physical space. You don't see Jesus spending the budget on lights and walls; he taught outside.

#37 Stock Toilet Paper

Okay, this post is not for the faint of heart. It's rated PG. Read on at your own risk.

Ever gone into your own bathroom at home, sat down...only to discover someone didn't restock the toilet paper? Crap. (That was bad, huh?) The tissue is in the hall closet. So you do the only thing you can do: you yell for someone to bring you a roll of toilet paper. Simple. You're home. With people you love. It happens.

Now, consider the same scenario with a guest at your church. Go ahead. Play this out. Your guest is in the restroom stall. There is no toilet paper. They check their pockets for a used tissue. Nothing. They reach under a wall, trying to find the roll in the adjacent stall. No luck. Now they're desperate. They consider the bulletin in their hand. No.

This isn't home. He or she doesn't know where the stock is. And if they did, they can't get to it from their stall trap. They're not going to yell for help. Who'd hear them? They're stuck. They're just stuck.

So your facility care team is cleaning the restroom on Monday and they find this embarrassed, maybe angry, tired soul stuck in stall number two. And if they did find a way out of the restroom, they may never come back. Not to the restroom, but to your church.

First impressions are lasting impressions.

Stock toilet paper. Stock an extra roll. Or two.

Oh, and by the way, provide two-ply, not the cheap one-ply stuff. That's about as bad as no tissue at all.

#38 Learn From the Marketplace

People are people and value is value. This is true outside the church as well as within the local church. Pay attention to what businesses and service organizations are doing well.

- Read books: anything from Disney, Nordstrom, and Starbucks.
- Read magazines like Fast Company, Forbes, and Wired.
- Visit airports, museums, and shopping malls—places with high traffic. Study signage and traffic flow.
- Pay attention to quality experiences in restaurants, hotels, airlines, and banks. What made it an exceptional experience?
- Play at Disney and other "experiential" venues. Pay attention to value-added touches that make the experience unique and memorable.

I wish this chapter wasn't in a best practices book for churches. I wish we didn't need to look at marketplace entities to learn how to value people. After all, we should be the leaders on this one. Following Jesus' way should make us intuitively the best at loving, the most creative at caring, the most innovative at communicating personal value. We should have the corner on this market.

My prayer is that one day it will all be right-sized and the marketplace will look at the local church and say, "The relationship with our customer is critical to our bottom line, our bottom dollar. So we must study, watch, and learn from the local church. They understand people. They get relationships. They communicate authentic value. They are our model."

Until then, continue to find truth wherever truth exists. Model personal value from wherever it's portrayed with excellence. Don't be afraid to learn from any and every one—even your local grocer, garage, or gadget expert.

WORST PRACTICE

Don't be influenced by any organization outside the church. What do they know? It's not like they bear the thumbprint of God or care about people the way you do.

HOW TO **WOW** YOUR CHURCH GUESTS

#39 Answer the Phone

This was almost laughable when we finally discovered it several years ago. We had answered the phone at our church throughout the week, addressing questions about service times and location frequently. Then on the weekends—the time when many people call, asking about service times and location—we had all our calls directed to voicemail. Sure, the caller could listen to a 47-option menu and find the recorded address and service time, but really...a recording when we had a hundred-plus guest services volunteers in the building?

Our phones are answered during all services on the weekend by a competent, gregarious, helpful volunteer. Simple.

Make a great first impression. Answer the phone with a live voice, especially on the weekends.

#40 | Brew Good Coffee

Our culture has quickly associated "free" with "cheap." "Cheap" is too often "garbage."

No church has to brew bad coffee. Even if it's free. Especially if you charge for it.

Value excellence. Value people. Value the brew.

If you're brewing coffee, don't make it "church" coffee.

'Nough said.

#41 | Keep It Clean

Cleanliness matters.

Cut the grass. Clean the parking lot. Shampoo the carpet. Shine the glass. Paint the walls. Stock the tissue. Pick up the trash. Straighten the chairs. Disinfect the drinking fountain.

Whether you see it, need it, or care about it isn't the point. Your guests see it. And it communicates value...or a lack of it.

#42   Imitate Jesus' Attitude

Read Philippians 2:5-11:

"In your relationships with one another, have the same mindset as
    Christ Jesus:

Who, being in very nature God,
    did not consider equality with God something to be used to his
    own advantage;
rather, he made himself nothing
    by taking the very nature of a servant,
    being made in human likeness.
And being found in appearance as a man,
    he humbled himself
    by becoming obedient to death—
    even death on a cross!

Therefore God exalted him to the highest place
    and gave him the name that is above every name,
that at the name of Jesus every knee should bow,
    in heaven and on earth and under the earth,
and every tongue acknowledge that Jesus Christ is Lord,
    to the glory of God the Father."

Here the Bible tells us that serving with Jesus' attitude means...

- setting one's own agenda aside for the sake of others.
- trading personal preferences for profound inconveniences.
- prioritizing others' interests...interests? Yeah, interests.
- being willing to not only serve, but be known as a servant.
- surrendering to the Father's kingdom agenda of love.

Here it is:

Position descriptions for staff and volunteers will always state the task as the job, but every job must be developed on this foundation: operate from Jesus' point of view. Perform with his mindset. Live out this attitude of love, respect, and humility.

Imitate Jesus.

Period.

WORST PRACTICE

Don't get hung up trying to figure out how Jesus handled guest services. He never took up an offering, parked a car, or showed someone around the Temple. He did drive money-changers from the Temple. Imitate that. There's some attitude!

#43 | Communication's Critical

Develop a plan to inform and inspire your teams.

• Inform:

> Communicate the schedule.
>> • Don't assume grown adults will remember. Life happens. Priorities are stacked. Be proactive.
>> • Print the schedule. Mail it. E-mail it. Post it. Then send it again.

> Make sure your volunteer leaders and teams have firsthand information.
>> • Let them know a baptism celebration is coming before it's printed in the bulletin.
>> • Invite them to participate in the vision process before the rest of the church.
>> • Give them feedback on what God's doing to change lives.

> Be clear about expectations.
>> • You want each person to be on time. Say so
>> • You have some expectations about attire. Be clear.
>> • You want each person to be uniquely wired to serve people. Define who that is up front.

• Inspire:

> Communicate the why behind what is being done.
>> • Vision is the why.
>> • A vision that's compelling is always inspiring.

> Tell stories.
>> • Acknowledge best practices. Be specific. Tell stories about the people who are nailing those practices.
>> • Celebrate outcomes of your team's service. Specify every hit and home run.

> Build relationships.
>> • See past the team to individuals.
>> • Invest personally with your time, your energy, your interest.
>> • Ask your team how you can pray for them. Follow up.

#44 See the Glass Half Full

Bring optimists onto your teams—people who see the best in life and other people. You've experienced the opposite. You've encountered the pessimist in the grocery store checkout line.

- "Only another hour and I'm outta here!"
- "They (the management, fellow employees, the gods) are never around when you need them."
- No eye contact, no expression, no greeting, hardly a goodbye.

Not only do optimists refrain from negative comments about the world as they see it, they also take great joy in finding things to celebrate.

- "Did you see the sunrise this morning?" (it's been raining since 7:30)
- "That's a great color on you." (they're color-blind and you're wearing black)
- "It's going to work out just fine." (about nearly anything).

Okay, maybe the optimism can be over the top, but you get my point. People who are looking for the best in people, in their day, in their world, are people who weigh in with Paul. Remember his letter to the Philippians?

"Summing it all up, friends, I'd say you'll do best by filling your minds and meditating on things true, noble, reputable, authentic, compelling, gracious—the best, not the worst; the beautiful, not the ugly; things to praise, not things to curse." (Philippians 4:8, The Message)

Optimists are contagious, but then again, so are pessimists. Choose well. How your teams and guests are influenced depends on your willingness to invite appropriately-wired people onto your guest services teams.

Fill that glass full.

#45 | Plan the Understated

I'm fascinated when I watch behind-the-scenes documentaries of movies, theme parks, or events. Sometimes it's the big, amazing, OMGosh, how'd-they-do-that scenes that grab me. Often it's the less significant, simple nuances that are, well, amazing.

This list isn't outstanding. You don't have to announce any of these. There's not much of a budget in this list. But someone had to plan. And the plan really matters.

- Keep the paper towels and tissue stocked.
- Add hand lotion in the restroom—especially during winter months.
- Be sensitive to flu fears: provide hand sanitizer.
- Print in readable fonts.
- Clean the carpet and other flooring.
- Set the thermostat.
- Make seating comfortable.
- Build an engaging greeter team.
- Keep the website up to date.
- Clear the snow.
- Wipe up spills
- Staff a competent children's team of volunteers.
- Put song words on the screen.
- Polish the drinking fountain.
- Spray air freshener.
- Clear the geese droppings (you can't shoot 'em; you can clean up after them).
- Block direct blinding sunlight.

Add to your own list. Think behind the scenes. Plan the understated.

WORST PRACTICE

You don't have time to pay attention to details. Stick to the big picture. Basics. If people need pampering, they can go to the spa. Besides, if people get the notion you really care, there'll be no end to their expectations.

#46 Buy an Umbrella

I love it when servant leaders—volunteers—co-own the ministry as entrepreneurial zealots.

The initial idea came from Mike, a volunteer greeter, who asked, "What if we replaced our too few, overused umbrellas with new, matching, logo-labeled umbrellas? Could we do that?" Eagerly, I asked him to please do the research and get back to me.

A few weeks later, Mike and several greeter friends escorted me to their own project. They had taken it upon themselves to not only research, but to raise funds from among their guest services peers and purchase 25 golf umbrellas bearing our church logo.

Never mind who funds the project. Buy some umbrellas. It's a little step. It's a lot of WOW.

#47 | Don't Just Fix It

Ownership is a powerful dynamic in any organization: people see a problem, they just fix it. No questions or squabbles about whose job is whose. No arguments about who gets the credit. The problem, large or small, gets fixed when it's identified.

That's all really good—to a point.

However, in addition to a culture of "can-do" ownership, there must be a feedback loop established. Otherwise, you'll have teams of people who continue to fix the same things over and over and over. A feedback loop will help you see patterns—system breakdowns, broken processes, little incidentals—that can be addressed and fixed for the long haul. Fixes that become preventative and habitual, not reactionary.

A feedback loop is merely a system that outlines clear communication and responsibility. Feedback about a broken fixture, missing information, or clunky system can be communicated via a Web service, e-mail, text, or phone. Once the issue is communicated, a designated person or team acts to solve the problem permanently. Ownership with a feedback process will result in positive change—not over and over, but consistently and permanently.

Don't just fix it.

WORST PRACTICE

Don't fix it at all. Let the paint chip, the carpet roll up, and the ice accumulate. People just need to see Jesus. Get over it.

#48 Everyone Has One

Our mission at Granger is "helping people take their next step toward Christ...together." Ultimately, I want journey-minded people on my team. People who...

- understand we're all on a spiritual journey toward God.
- embrace the mission to create an atmosphere conducive to taking steps toward Christ.
- accept their role in the process: create a safe place, extend accepting relationships, affirm people right where they are.
- are clearly focused on others because their search matters, and because their Creator says they matter.

Technique, personality, professionalism aside—people who understand that individuals are on personal journeys toward Christ will contagiously impact the team's focus and morale. These folks will help carry and communicate the vision.

People who are on a mission—your agreed-upon mission—will energize your team and keep first things first for guests. Everyone has a next step.

#49 | Kill the Rules

I hate rules. Most rules, that is. Rules that ostracize. Rules that alienate. Rules that create outsiders to the club, to the business, or to the church. I hate those rules.

In fact, most of us hate those rules. And we know an "offing" rule when we see one. We interpret rules as rules even when the organization or person doesn't call it a "rule." When we hear policy from a company, we think rules. When we read the fine print on a contract, we think rules. When we hear repeated expectations from a spouse, boss, or a peer, we hear rules.

Generally speaking again, rules seem to repel us. We feel confined, closed in, limited. Now, don't go theological on me just yet. I'm not suggesting that rules don't have their place. Fact is, many rules serve a good purpose in expressing commitment and respect.

For instance, in the medical field there are red rules and blue rules.

- Red rules can't be broken. Rules like: "Nothing is to be administered to a patient without first consulting the patient's chart." Now, the rule can be broken, but at the risk of the life of the patient and/or the employee's job. Red rules. You can't break 'em without dire circumstances.
- Blue rules are in place to assist in creating a smooth operation. Rules like: "The shift schedule is to be placed on the bulletin board at the nurses' station, left of the visitor check-in chart." No one's going to die or lose their job if this rule gets broken, but it'll create a little frustration for people. It's a blue rule. There's a reason for it, but it can be bent...even broken.

Here's the challenge: Every church has rules.

- No running in the halls.
- No drinks or food in the auditorium.
- We call the big room where we meet for services the "sanctuary," not the "auditorium."

- No jeans in the service.
- We always use the KJV in the public reading of the Bible.
- No parking at the curbside.
- No use of the center auditorium (or sanctuary or worship center or whatever you call it) doors after the service prelude.

Here's the question: Do your people, do your guest services teams know which rules are red and which rules are blue?

- What's at stake if a child runs with sheer delight toward the 4-year-old room?
- What's the worst thing that can happen if a guest takes a cup of coffee into the service?
- Is it okay to use a word like *auditorium* that everyone is familiar with?
- Do guests know they can wear whatever is comfortable to your church? Can they?

You get the point. Now, here's the deal. You may have some expectations in place for very good reasons, but if there's confusion about which rules are red and which rules are blue, your people will likely "enforce" the rules as red. And when they do, your guests—new people and members alike—will bristle.

They hate rules, too.

Review your expectations for everything: with your teams, with your staff, with your board.

- What's red? What will risk life or the honor of God?
- What's blue? What makes things more efficient...but really doesn't risk life or the honor of God?

Then communicate what really matters and focus on loving people, not the rules we want them to observe in order to be one of us.

#50 | Play Some Tunes

Emotion, a journal of the American Psychological Association, reported on the positive effects of music in a 2008 study with 32 college students in Sweden. Happiness/elation and nostalgia/longing were more likely to be experienced when listening to music than when students were not listening to music.

Most of us do not need a psych study to affirm the uplifting effects of music on our general state of mind. While most of us don't consciously consider whether our mood is enhanced by listening to tunes, most of us would agree that music playing in our car, home, office, or earbuds at least reflects our emotional feelings, most likely improving our mood.

If our general experience and psychological studies verify the benefits of music, why not have some tunes playing when people walk into your building or drive onto your campus? Music sets a tone. It communicates something is happening. In the mall, a restaurant, and at your church, music—even background music—sets up the environment and helps people experience a boost emotionally. All that's true, given you play music that's uplifting. Play some angry Nine Inch Nails or a funeral hymn, and you'll project a very different mood—one that may agitate or depress your guests. Music is powerful.

Create a playlist that lifts, and welcome your guests with music.

#51 Build an "I've Been Here" Space

We've done some informal surveys and discovered that when people decide to go to church for the first time (or to go to church again after years of not attending anywhere), they often do so with a fair amount of fear. They have not-so-fond memories, or they've heard stuff through pop media, and they enter our church—or any church—with a fair amount of hesitation.

- How will I know where to go?
- Will they ask for my money?
- How will I know when to sit, stand, or kneel?
- Will I be the only "normal" person there?

We want every person who decides to attend our church—especially those filled with fear and apprehension—to feel welcome and accepted. We want them to know we expected them; we've prepared for them.

We want our guests to feel "at home." We want them to experience "familiar." We want them to be able to drop guards and fears that keep them from experiencing the wonder of God's love through the message of Jesus Christ.

So consider this: many of our guests—our focused audience—walk into Starbucks (or the coffee shop of their choice), order, and pay for their own coffee/drink 3-7 times per week or more. They know it. It's familiar. They've "been there before."

When a guest walks into our church, they smell the aroma of coffee, they see a "Starbucks-esque" cafe...and they know exactly what to do. It's easy, it's familiar...they feel at home. The questions of "what to do when" are suspended for the moment. Once the edge is off, there's space for taking the place in, getting acclimated, even sharing a conversation.

It's a crazy social phenomenon: when a guest—or anyone—gets a 12-ounce cup of anything in their hand, they're more relaxed. They have something to do with their hands. And if others in that space are also enjoying a beverage, they feel "normal." Even burly, 6-foot-3-inch men can hide behind a cup of coffee or a bottle of water!

Fears subside. Our guest is experiencing a social norm for themselves in our environment. There's a sense that they've "been here before."

If the rest of the experience—God's love shared through warm smiles, engaging conversation, and accepting welcomes—is on target, our guests will sense that they matter to God and to us, and they'll enter our services open to the message.

What can you do to help your guests feel they've "been here before?"

WORST PRACTICE

Make church as uncomfortable as possible. It's supposed to be different. When people don't know how to act, it throws them off balance. Now we've got 'em!

#52 | Change It

Best practices risk becoming mundane routines when they are not frequently evaluated for effectiveness and relevance. "Because we've always done it this way" isn't a good enough reason to keep doing it the same way.

Eight years into the same team scheduling process, we stopped to evaluate whether or not the rotation plan was still fulfilling our objectives. We had established a six-week rotation schedule for our volunteer teams, asking them to serve all evening Saturday and all morning Sunday. Our goal was to enhance the sense of community that could be developed by serving an entire weekend together. We also believed the same team serving throughout the weekend would serve our guests with greater consistency.

When we finally stopped to evaluate the effectiveness of our scheduling, we found that a month and half between serving together was actually a deterrent to community. We also discovered that gradual shifts over time meant that not every team member was serving all weekend long. Our rotation schedule no longer served our objectives.

Eight years. What came to be normal was actually a rut preventing us from maximizing community and effective guest service.

We changed it.

Sometimes change should happen because something is ineffective or broken. Other times you should change it before the practice, habit, or system becomes commonplace. Commonplace breeds complacency, and complacency breeds ineffectiveness.

We risk loving our systems more than the potential outcome of those systems. Think first of people. Build systems and processes that serve people, not the other way around.

Maybe you like the occasional "limited-time only" McRib sandwich from McDonald's. I don't. McDonald's does burgers. Smokey Bones does ribs. Montgomery Steakhouse does ribs. When McDonald's offers ribs, it's just disappointing to me. It's not their strength.

Does that mean your church should compare its ministries to the ministries of every other church in town and stop doing what someone else is doing better? Maybe. It'd sure kill a lot of redundancies. But, no, that's not the point.

Lean into what you do well. Got an awesome kids' program? Make it even better! Have gifted teachers? Create a platform for them to communicate!

As an individual, you have strengths, too. Hone those. Get better. Lead the way with what God's gifted you to do. Don't settle for "good enough." Blow the top off. It's what Paul encouraged young Timothy to do:

"For this reason I remind you to fan into flame the gift of God, which is in you through the laying on of my hands." (2 Timothy 1:6)

#54 | Talk Normal

One Monday morning I made several visits at a local hospital. One patient tried to tell me about his prognosis in the terms his doctor had used. We were both lost. The medical terms were over both our heads. Ultimately, he understood that one more minor surgical procedure would have him on his way home. We both knew what that meant. It was worth celebrating.

Most organizations are guilty of it: using insider language that's common for insiders, but foreign to those outside or new to the organization. When I was in the employment and training field, acronyms were our favorite mode of communication. We didn't intend it to be insider code, it was just our vocabulary.

I don't think we intend to use code or insider language in our local churches, either—but we do.

- Local churches tend to label ministries with snappy, fun names that don't help guests understand what it really is.
  - For a long time we used labels like Oasis and Lifeline, but then changed the name to Granger Student Ministries to describe what it really is.
  - Call a class a class, a group a group, a service a service.
- Churches tend to call their weekend handouts "bulletins."
  - Why not call it a program? That's what people normally call a handout at a concert, play, or ballgame.
- Words like "serve" can sound intimidating.
  - Inviting people to "volunteer" is familiar language that everyone understands.
- Words like "testimony" conjure up images of a courtroom.
  - Why not just use words like "story" to talk about someone's journey or life change?

- The church service often takes place in the "worship center" or the "sanctuary."
  - Almost everyone understands "auditorium" as a gathering place. Is the function of the room important enough to risk confusion for new guests?

What language needs to be changed in your local church or organization that would help guests better relate to your culture and message?

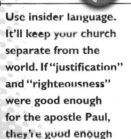

WORST PRACTICE

Use insider language. It'll keep your church separate from the world. If "justification" and "righteousness" were good enough for the apostle Paul, they're good enough for us.

#55 | You're Not Superman

I've met so many pastors and ministry directors who conceal their Superman cape, but lead people with a big "S" on their chest. Their span of care is literally 20, 30, 60 people. They attempt to lead large groups of people with little to no help. They haven't invested in future leaders. One thing is for sure: the "S" on their chest doesn't represent "smart."

When your span of care is too broad, people won't experience your care. You won't have time to shepherd. You'll likely communicate poorly. Operate with an out-of-control span of care long enough and all you'll do is run around trying to solve problems that are created by poor leadership.

Look instead at Jesus' life. He chose to invest his life into only 12 disciples. He chose three of those to invest deeper still. Jesus was a "super" man. You're not. Get over yourself and share leadership. You'll care more effectively when you do.

#56 Everyone Can Greet

At first the notion that everyone can greet flies in the face of what I train and coach—with our own people and leaders of other churches. A warm body, even a warm smiling body, just isn't enough. There's a unique wiring that people-people—wow-makers—possess. Make no compromises.

However, the only people greeting guests should *not be limited* to your greeters or other guest services team members. Your guests may see the occasional "official" nametag on an usher, hospitality host, or greeter; however, those volunteers and staff aren't the only people your guests will see—or interact with. A warm, inclusive, accepting greeting is a warm, inclusive, accepting greeting regardless of who's giving it.

Consider Ruth Saratore's story from Granger Community Church.

I attended Ruth's funeral as another Granger pastor led the service. Ruth was 88 years old. Always sat on the second row, left side of the center aisle. Every Sunday. Ruth wasn't one of those people who felt she owned that seat. She never protected it. Instead, she was constantly inviting people to sit *with* her.

Matt spoke at Ruth's funeral. His story? Five years prior he entered Granger for the first time. Alone, tentative, looking for a seat. He made it down front early one Sunday and heard the sweetest sound. It was Ruth. "Are you alone young man? Sit right here with me." No, Ruth wasn't hitting on him. She was in her eighties. He was barely 30 (I know it happens, but she was no cougar, believe me). At the end of the service, she told him, "I'll be here next week. I hope you come back. I'll be saving a seat for you."

That was enough for Matt. Granger was his church. Ruth was his friend. He was home.

Several more people revealed the same "sit with me" story. Stories that continued beyond the weekend service. Ruth made phone calls during the week. Her new friends dropped by for weekday visits. Ruth extended herself to serve and love others.

She never wore a nametag. She didn't volunteer at the guest relations center. She wasn't a greeter (although she could have been).

But she greeted—warmly and inclusively. Ruth was unconditionally accepting.

Guests don't really care who warmly receives them. You don't need a label or a tag. They just care that someone cares.

Everyone can greet.

- Build a culture in your church where greeting people you don't know is normal.
- Make it unacceptable for members to talk only with their church friends.
- Implement the "three and five" rule. The team at Foothills Community Church in Seneca, SC ask their people to speak with three people they don't know for the first five minutes after the service.
- Offer a time in the service for people to turn and greet each other. You may be surprised how that simple handshake and "hello" impacts a new person.

Develop a culture of inclusiveness where your guest services teams aren't the only people who are nice to guests. Anyone can greet! Anyone.

#57 Keep It Simple

Keep it all simple. All of it.

- Don't overdo the signage. Make it big. Make it clear. Make it matter.

- Limit the on-ramps. Don't announce/promote everything going on in your church. When everything has the same perceived importance, nothing is more important than anything else. Invite new guests to limited, practical, accessible, visible next steps. The fewer the better.

- Provide a bulletin or program, not a weekly multi-piece magazine filled with flyers

- Meet people where they are—not where you wish they were. Right now they're just asking where the men's room is. Help them with that.

- Avoid churchy words and phrases in your print pieces. Use "normal" language. You want people to understand clearly, not be impressed by your Christianese. Write simply. Write like a "normal" person.

- Empower your teams to simply serve, to practice the golden rule. It's what Jesus taught. It should be sufficient for you.

- Provide easy-to-read words for songs. Don't require a lot of page turning through multiple books in order to keep up with the service.

WORST PRACTICE

"Simple" dumbs down the Gospel. Don't apologize for your complex, religiously worded theology, a place called Zion, or that Ebenezer thing you keep raising when you sing.

#58 | Collaborate

Many of my dealings with my cell phone company remind me that systems are often developed for ease within an organization—with little regard to the guest who is trying to navigate the twists and turns, hoping for a satisfactory solution at the end of the ride. After being passed from one department to another, it becomes apparent that no single department or staffer is empowered to cross department lines and offer the help longed for. The right hand doesn't know what the left hand is doing. Jesus said that works well when it comes to selfless giving, but I don't think it applies to the cell phone company—or your church's service to your guests.

When expertise gets relegated to experts behind department walls and team lines, the guest is left wandering through a frustrating maze of smoke and mirrors. Even in the church world.

Inform your teams. Share ideas. Connect your teams by radio so communication is easy and immediate. Get your children's team and guest services team together to brainstorm best practices. Work in partnership with your arts team to communicate one message—before guests experience the service.

Collaborate. Speak with one voice. Minimize the maze.

#59 Standardize

While every guest is unique and deserves to be treated as such, finding ways to standardize responses and processes will allow you to:

- Speak with one voice
  - ➤ Take the guesswork out of common questions. Make sure the entire team is informed with basic information about core ministries, children's rooms, current events, and where to find essentials like values, vision, and statement of faith.

- Simplify training for new team members
  - ➤ What are the rudimentary skills required of every person? What best practices are vital for an excellent guest experience? Train everyone with the same baseline, from the parking lot to the guest services desk.

- Streamline the communication loop
  - ➤ How do guests make prayer requests? How do they make comments and provide feedback? Create simple, clear pathways for guests to communicate with you.

#60 Celebrate Excellence

When I experience an appetite-suppressing, nauseating restroom at a restaurant, I consider the entire staff to be negligent. I don't really care whose job it is to clean—someone, anyone, everyone on the team should care enough about the guest's experience to get a bucket and some Lysol and get busy!

When someone at your church, or mine, can't find the right kid's room or finds no tissue in the restroom or trips over the rolled-up doormat—someone on the guest services team should spring into action. In fact, if the right people are on your team—people who see, hear, and feel excellence or the lack of it—they will see that these experiences don't happen. They'll anticipate, be on the lookout, and work a plan to see that every guest who needs help is assisted, the tissue is stocked, and the doormat is flat.

Some things you can teach. You can train someone to answer the phone, you can show someone how to use the database system, you can help someone listen more actively. People *can* be taught what to watch for and how to prevent service delivery gaps. However, if they don't appreciate excellence—if they don't understand that it honors God and inspires people—they'll only work off the list you give them. They'll watch the tissue stock, the wandering family, and the doormat. But they may miss other opportunities for improvement. They may miss the traffic congestion, the ringing phone, or the spilled coffee.

WORST PRACTICE

Don't expect too much from your volunteers. Perfection is impossible. Excellence is arrogant. Actually, don't expect much at all.

Excellence champions think of people. They think about experiences. They understand what it is to communicate value to people through excellent experiences. So they anticipate, they prevent, they own the opportunity—and the problem.

#61 Learn From Your Own Experiences

You've read about a number of my personal experiences in this book already. Each time I encounter an impersonal sales associate, I reflect on the warmth of our guest services teams. Every time I experience systems that serve the company but leave me, the customer, lost in the abyss of red tape, I review our own communication loop. When I find myself confused over insider language in another organization, I listen more carefully to the words and catchphrases that roll off our churched tongue without thinking.

Read all you can. Practice the golden rule. And pay attention to your own customer service experiences. Note your impulsive reaction. Do you feel angry? Devalued? Ignored? Irritated? Disconnected? Warm and fuzzy? Heard? Appreciated?

Consider the emotive responses from your church guests when they ask questions and don't get consistent answers, or they expect a return call that never comes, or they feel confused and "outside" the system created for the ease of the church staff.

Consider. And learn. Create best practices from your own experiences that help you honor people as God sees them.

#62　Model

Jason Hester, former executive pastor of ministries at Pinelake Church in Brandon, MS, lived this every weekend. When he walked into their commons, he went into action, rather than telling others what to do. If a children's volunteer didn't show up, he stepped into the chaos and rocked babies. By doing so, Jason communicated several things to his teams:

- I'm not asking you to do anything I am not willing to do.

- I value what you're doing, enough to come alongside you and join you.

- You do what I do: step in where you're needed. Care for people—volunteers and guests—in the moment.

Managing often requires something of others. Leading models for others. Don't be afraid to pass out a program, staff the front door, check in some children, or wipe down a sink. When you do, you'll begin to understand and experience servant leadership.

#63 Use Spell-Check

In 2010, one of our local school districts made a horribly embarrassing mistake. A major typo. I do mean major. Not in an inner-office memo. Not in a school handbook. The school district misspelled a word on a larger-than-life billboard by leaving out the "l" in "public."

People notice misspellings. On billboards and in church bulletins. Mistakes don't have to be mortifying mistakes to communicate a lack of thoroughness and excellence. Simple typos create distractions from the message you're trying to communicate.

Use spell-check and a proofreader (or two).

WORST PRACTICE

Don't get caught up in detales like layout, graphiks or speling. People need to here your message, not applaud your profing.

#64 Control and Correct

You need to address every problem. But timing is everything. What if your teams and leaders understood this simple distinction?

On Sunday, you are responsible for controlling only three things: your smile, your response to challenges, and the value you place on the people impacted by the challenge. That's it. Three things. You can't fix it on Sunday. You deal with it, you can respond to it, but you likely can't correct it.

On Monday, you can correct it.

In that order. Control. Correct. You'll have to get through it on Sunday. But you'll need a long-term solution—a best practice—so everyone understands how to respond the next time "it" happens.

Control your attitude on Sunday. Correct on Monday. That's what Jason Hester (former executive pastor of ministries at Pinelake) tells his team.

#65 Watch the Clock

This is a known best practice for every leader and team member outside the worship center or auditorium. Those leading the service sometimes struggle to adhere to it. This is not a directive on the required length of your service. Meet for an hour, seventy minutes, two hours; that's up to you. But, communicate value and care to everyone involved.

TrueNorth's Mike Fiedler notes: "While we all need to leave margin for the Holy Spirit to speak through our teaching pastor, the reality is that when the check-in and check-out process bottlenecks in our children's areas, frustration mounts in everyone." Everyone outside feels the pain of a service that should have ended ten, fifteen, twenty minutes ago. Your parking attendants, the children's teams, your ushers and greeters—everyone is stretched.

And don't forget your guests. Yes, God may have spoken during the service, but as our senior pastor, Mark Beeson, often reminds us: "The mind can only absorb what the seat can endure."

#66 | Have a Baby Plan

Not a small plan. Not a tiny plan. You need to have a plan to care for and respond to babies, and their parents, in your service. Screaming babies are a clear distraction to guests in your service. But there's also nothing cuter (or more diverting) than an adorable, cooing child.

Babies matter to God, no doubt. But so do the adults sitting around them who can't hear what God's saying through the arts or the message because of the innocent, expressive child.

Have a plan:

- A place for parents to take their children and still participate in the service. Maybe it's a "cry room." Maybe it's a café or a lobby with a TV monitor to view the service.
- Offer assistance to parents before the service. Show them the alternative space you provide for children. Communicate that the space exists because you value the experience of children. You want them to learn they matter to God in an age-appropriate manner.
- Train your teams to discreetly and sensitively invite parents out of the service to the alternative space you've provided.
- Follow-up after the service to answer questions, provide more information, and communicate value to the entire family.

This will be one of the toughest practices to exercise. It requires lots of grace. And then a little bit more.

WORST PRACTICE

Someone have the guts to do what many people want: start a church for adults only.

Kim Hogue, assimilation director for Koinonia Christian Fellowship in Hanford, California, extends the notion of first impressions and guest services beyond their weekend into all their other gatherings. She leads the teams at KCF who take the following strategy with all their environments:

- Create environments: They consider the guests who'll occupy that space. Is this a person who was "dragged" to church, doesn't know Jesus, or isn't sure they buy the church gig? Is the gathering for people who are convinced of God's love and committed to following him? Consider the audience, then create the space.

- Challenge environments: There is constant evaluation of the impression being made in children's, students', women's, and other affinity-based gatherings. First impressions are first impressions.

- Change environments: When a setting needs to be altered to better speak to the needs and interests of those participating, they change it. Period.

#68 | Create Some Buzz

My budget's too small to eat everywhere I'd like to eat. My friends tell me I should be happy with Taco Bell, but I really get excited about a dining experience that brings together exquisite culinary talent with compelling atmosphere and personal service. But that usually means I read about such WOW experiences.

Jackie Huba, who writes for the blog Church of the Customer, cites two restaurants (French Laundry and Cyrus—both in Northern California) to illustrate five ways to compete with a bigger and more dominant competitor. Number three on her list grabbed my attention. Here's how she puts it:

"Do something buzz-worthy in the first few minutes. As the Cyrus hostess leads you from the bar/reception area, she stops just inside the dining room. There, she picks up a white Zsa-Zsa telephone and says into it: 'Chef, the McConnell party is here for table 42. Please send someone out to greet them.' It's startling and unexpected. Who calls the chef to say a guest has arrived? It was great theater."

So what's happening in your church that's buzz-worthy in the first few minutes? What has people leaning over in the first few minutes of the service—or better yet, on their way into the service—and whispering, "Wow"?

The competition isn't the church around the corner. The competition is anywhere your guest has experienced a WOW that has created buzz around them. Our opportunity in creating buzz is to get people talking about the local church, and get them talking about Christ with an enthusiasm that is authentic and organic—because it's based on their WOW experience. The reality is that "evangelists" are often created from folks who are still kicking the tires, still checking out the claims of Christ. They invite their friends because the buzz is bringing them back.

And that buzz? It's all about value. It's all about personal care. People begin to get it: they matter. They matter to God, and they matter to us.

That's worth creating some buzz.

What's the buzz factor around your community about your church?

#69 Remember Your First Time

It's easy to forget. We forget what it was like to walk in alone. We forget not knowing where the restroom is. We don't think about the fears we carried into church years ago. We're home now. It's all too familiar.

Katie Czapala, volunteer coordinator at TrueNorth Church in North Augusta, South Carolina encourages leaders to go visit other churches. Alone. And then she adds, "rinse and repeat." Go visit. Make note of the awkwardness. Be aware of what you don't know. How do you wish people would treat you…or not treat you?

Then "rinse and repeat." Get in the habit of driving onto your church site using the eyes of the new person. Engage people without focusing on what you hope they hear from you, but intent on what you can understand from them.

Remember your first time.

#70 | Tell Stories

Tim Keel wrote: "Throughout history people have told stories and been shaped by them, and in doing so they have discovered and constructed ways of understanding who they are and what is happening in the world around them."

The numbers on your weekend service tally sheet represent faces. Faces of men and women and children. And every one of those faces holds stories. Personal and real stories. And while we may not get the opportunity to engage in all the details with folks on the weekend, we will walk away with some of their stories.

On one weekend alone, I heard stories—albeit shortened versions—of personal pain, deep loss, enormous joy, and quiet peace. I heard the story of a man who was literally dying; the cancer would take his life in just a few weeks. Another man told me the heart-wrenching but inspiring story of his 35-year-old brother who died just a week prior. I celebrated with a man who started a new job that week—after being out of work for a year. I needed to hear those stories as much as those sharing needed to tell their stories. They help me look at my own life, and they help me take in what is really happening around me. They connect me to others and help me live outside my own little world.

I want our teams to hear stories like those. Stories that take us past the task. Past the rush of getting everyone into the service. Past the pace of a six-service weekend. Stories that cause us to pause and thank God for the people we get to encounter.

There are also other stories. Stories of our team members' God-moments with our guests. Moments that touched them. Moments that called the best out of them. Moments where they got to witness God at work—right in front of their eyes. Everyone needs to hear those stories. Stories that help us "get it." Get that God is using us right here, right now.

America's authority on storytelling, Robert McKee, put it this way: "Stories are the creative conversion of life itself into a more powerful, clearer, more meaningful experience. They are the currency of human contact."

Tell stories. And perhaps more importantly, listen to the stories of others. It is the ultimate human contact.

#71 | Diversify

There's a common leadership principle that suggests we attract who we are. John Maxwell calls it the Law of Magnetism. If you completely understand this "law," you'll realize that leaders must work hard to add people to their team who don't necessarily mirror themselves.

Here's at least one application of this law in the world of guest services in your local church or organization. You have a dyno-leader who's 62. Professional in every way. Sharp image. Mature leadership. Formal, but personable presentation. This leader will naturally attract others like her. That's not a bad thing. Just know she will.

The leader of another team is 24 years old. Sharp, but hip. Untucked shirt, frayed jeans, no socks. Mature leader. Laid back and personable. He will attract others like himself. And that's not a bad thing either. Just know it will happen.

Each of these leaders will attract other competent people like themselves. There's room for all of them. However, watch how this unfolds.

Each of these leaders directs a greeter team on different weekends. Which means on weekend one, when the mature 62-year-old is leading, the majority of team members greeting at doors and assisting guests are mature 60-somethings. Again, there's nothing wrong with that, except that there will likely be younger people attending the service this weekend. When they arrive, they might assume, "I don't know if this is my church, because..." don't miss this... "there's no one here like me."

The same thing will happen next week when the team is comprised of 20- and 30-somethings. Older people will arrive and wonder if this church is their church, because "everyone seems younger."

People want to fit in. They want to sense that they belong. Remove those potential barriers. Diversify your teams.

Your leaders will have to work hard to do so. They'll have to empower other younger—or older—team members to invite and involve others like them. Then when guests arrive, on any weekend, they'll sense at first glance that they just might belong.

#72 | Value Your Volunteers

Gonna keep this simple. It seems like a no-brainer, yet it's so easy to miss opportunities to value volunteers who lead and carry the ministry of your church. Here are some ideas:

- Bake a cake! We have volunteer leaders who do that for their team of volunteers (or they pick it up at the local market)—just because.
- Send a note—after the weekend service.
- Thank them face-to-face.
- Cast vision as you thank them—remind them why they do what they do...why it matters at all.
- Demonstrate that you're happy to see them!
- Empower them with responsibility for the ministry. Let them make decisions.
- Take time to coach them. Invest in them. Believe in them.
- Provide serving roles of significance. Make it worth their time and energy.
- Thank them publicly. During a service.
- Throw a party!
- Don't expect them to be "lifers." Give them an opportunity to "re-up."
- Brag on them to other volunteers.
- Brag on them to other volunteers in front of the volunteer you're bragging about.
- Ask about their lives. And care enough to listen.

WORST PRACTICE

Don't go out of your way to pat volunteers on the back. They're doing exactly what they should be doing—giving their lives away. They should be sacrificing. They should be tired. Don't acknowledge or celebrate them. Last thing you need are puffed-up volunteers.

- Remember what they told you...and follow-up.
- Pray for them.
- Trust them to pray for you.
- Build relationships.
- Develop reasonable spans of care, so you really *can* care and people really experience it.

#73 Create a Schedule

I learned the hard way. People need to be reminded.

Back in my student ministry days (days and days and days ago), I thought that grown adults could remember meeting dates and times. After all, they get kids to soccer practice, keep doctor appointments, show up for work, and remember birthdays. All that's true. And maybe that's the point: it's ALL true. There's a lot going on.

People, even grown, responsible adults, forget.

It's happened to all of us.

Weekend service is here. You're ready. You're on time. And someone on your team isn't. Short-handed, you hobble through the service (or services) on a shoestring, hoping to not miss any critical elements or people as you attempt to provide a welcoming space for your guests. It happens. People aren't always blowing off responsibility. Sometimes people just forget.

Here are some thoughts about scheduling your team for maximum participation.

- Create a schedule. Put it on paper. Make sure everyone has it.

- Make the schedule easy to remember. Build some pattern into it. Monthly. Biweekly. Find a rhythm.

- Send reminders. Make phone calls. Send postcards. Tweet. Text. E-mail.

- And you must, you must, you must *NOT* choose the easiest and preferred communication for *yourself* as the leader. Learn how to most effectively communicate with each individual on your team. You'll likely call some, text others, and e-mail the rest.

- Follow up when someone doesn't show. This is a simple and opportune chance to care. You may discover they're facing difficulty, illness, or worse. Reach out. You made it past the weekend. That's good. But that's not all there is to the team. The team is made up of people, people who need care.

- Expect the schedule to be kept and followed. Let people hear you say, "We're counting on you!"

By planning, printing, reminding, and following up on the schedule, you'll communicate that people matter, including your team.

Sunday's coming! Is your team?

#74 Team Is More Than Task

Unfortunately, a team of people committed to a common task or cause can be so focused on that task that they forget they're doing it together. Our senior pastor, Mark Beeson, has reminded us often at Granger that we want to keep some kind of "balance" between task and relationship.

Any task worth accomplishing requires focus. Greeting guests, feeding the poor, teaching children—these and more require attention. It's easy when the pace is fast and the need is intense; we can be relentless about just "gitten' 'er dun." The risk is that we may miss the people with whom we're serving, and by doing so, miss half the benefit of serving as a team.

Consider the following contrasts of healthy tension between task and relationship in teams:

Task	Team
Vision helps the team know why they're doing the task	Values define how we'll perform the task with common norms
Competence is required to do the task well	Community celebrates uniqueness on the team
Expectations are communicated, ensuring we complete the task with excellence	Agreement is reached between leader and teammates, establishing trust
Empowerment allows the team to go about the task with confidence	Ownership means members will take responsibility not only for task, but each other
Evaluation is necessary to track effectiveness	Feedback loop ensures communication among the team is open at all times
Change will be the natural result of evaluation of past and vision of future	Stories help people embrace change and move through transition with the team
Coaching is about teaching, often focused on technique and skill sets	Modeling is about personal investment, valuing personal development

Let's get more practical. Here are some quick thoughts about maximizing relationships in the process of accomplishing the tasks of ministry:

- Build "connect" time into the serving time.
  - ➢ Expect volunteers to arrive early enough to eat together, pray together, and prepare for their service opportunities.

- If you're the leader of the team, make sure you're "free" during the serving time to talk, invest, and celebrate "wins."
  - ➢ If you allow yourself to get "stuck" in a task role, you'll not be available to do so.

- Extend the conversation beyond the serving component.
  - ➢ Using personal visits, e-mail, phone, Twitter, Facebook, or other social networking platforms, encourage the team to share life by supporting each other outside the weekend or other serving times.

- Initiate a mass e-mail follow-up to the serving time.
  - ➢ Send e-mails listing prayer concerns, praises, and news about team members and the next gathering or serving time.

- Remember birthdays, anniversaries, and other important high points in the lives of your team members.
  - ➢ Bake a cake. Send a card. Allow time for people to talk to each other about their day-to-day interests.

- Celebrate the "wins" of the task.

- Acknowledge that the team accomplished "X." Celebrate stories you've heard from guests and members to mark the effectiveness of the team.

What else are you doing to balance the tension between task and team?

#75 | Be in the Moment

Everyone arrives at your church campus under the same circumstances. Everyone. Your guests, your volunteer teams, your staff, you.

Someone in your home didn't feel like going to church on Sunday. You overslept. You were up too late the previous night. Before leaving the house, someone couldn't find their socks. You left late. You forgot something and had to go back. The kids were fighting. You were fighting. And you were stopped by a train. Besides, you still have a long list of unfinished items on your to-do list for the weekend.

The pastor, volunteers, you, me. We arrive at church easily distracted. Rushed and harried, our minds everywhere but in the present moment. Everywhere but "here." Right "here," right now.

Providing excellent guest service requires being present in the moment, every time.

And not just our own moment. Someone else's moment. And the next moment, and the next person's, and the next...

Here are some quick thoughts to help you stay engaged:

- Sleep the night before. (Radical, huh?)

- Awake with margin. To eat. To focus. To reflect on why you're going where you're going. (Now, it's serious.)

- Go early. The train is gonna be slow; it's a train. You'll likely be stopped by it.

- Meet with friends and/or your team well before you need to be where you're going to need to be. Debrief. Decompress. Pray. Get focused. (Believe me: you need their help.)

- Keep praying. Practice presence with Jesus.

- Read body language.

- Connect through your eyes, not merely your smile. (People can tell.)

- Ask questions. Enter into another person's world, if only for a moment.

- As your mind drifts back into your day, or forward into your day, stop. Set it aside. Come back. Be fully present.

- Engage people as Jesus would...as people who matter to God.

Be in the moment.

#76 Get Dressed!

It's just a good idea. Fully clothed greeters at the front doors of your church are more than helpful. And, of course, that's not exactly what I'm talking about here.

People will show up dressed. The question is, will they be dressed for your guests? And how will they know how to dress unless you tell them? No rocket science here. Someone needs to communicate the expectations, whatever they are.

Perhaps at first glance this sounds shallow or externally focused. Well, externally focused it is, shallow it is not.

The fact is, appearance matters when you're intentionally creating an atmosphere of hospitality. When most people invite new guests into their home, they will shower, fix their hair, look presentable, and clean the house. I'm not talking about "putting on airs"; I'm merely suggesting that your teams should "look" like they're expecting company.

Unfortunately, you have people in your church who don't understand "image." They're good people. They love Jesus. But they are as inappropriate for greeting guests as a tuneless person leading your music would be. Your guests are asking one of just a few questions as they approach your campus for the first time: "Are there others here like me?" or "Will I fit here?"

So some fashion sense is necessary. Some level of appropriate pride is needed. Without shifting their focus onto themselves as though serving is about them, I want people who look in the mirror before leaving the house fully aware that scores of people will see that reflected image today. And as they look in the mirror I want them to ask themselves, "Will people want to meet me today?"

At Granger, we expect our team members to...

- look in the mirror before they leave the house. Messy hair and crusty eyes are not welcoming.

- leave the Bud Lite T-shirt at home for mowing. Just not helpful at the front door of the church.
- dress modestly. We want people turned on to Jesus, if you know what I mean.
- be themselves. Use an iron if the shirt calls for it; don't if it doesn't.

The point is, communicate what you expect. Once your inappropriately dressed team member arrives to serve, it's a difficult conversation at best. You have four not-so-optimal choices to lay out for the ill-dressed volunteer (or staffer):

- Ask them to go home and change clothes. That might work if they live on the church property. Otherwise, that's a tough thing to ask.
- Tell them you've got a wardrobe of modest, clean options they can choose from. That's a fully stocked inventory of sizes and styles.
- Tell them they cannot serve today. Invite them to enjoy the service, knowing their teammates will ask them why they aren't serving. Awkward.
- Let them serve as they are. Forget about perceptions of your guests or inconsistencies with your team. That's a risk with future consequences you may not want.

Avoid all that. Not only should your teams get dressed, they should know what's expected.

Be clear and upfront. Clear communication communicates value.

WORST
PRACTICE

Don't communicate anything about attire. Let people be who they are. You can't police necklines, hem lengths, or tight clothing. Besides, when's the last time you told a guy how low his v-neck should be?

#77 | Bust Up Your Party

If you've read my book *First Impressions* or you've been in one of my workshops, you've heard me say this...and say this. I'll say it again.

Bust up your party!

Here's the scenario...fraught with tension: You and your greeter buds are near an entry, intending to greet guests as they enter your building or room. It's been at least seven days since you've all seen each other, maybe longer since you've volunteered together. You're having a great time laughing it up, swapping stories, catching up on life. This is community at its finest (or depending on your church culture and language: *fellowship* at it finest)!

And guests are just streaming by—"ungreeted."

Arggggh.

Here's the tension. We want community and relationship among our team members. However, we also want our guests to be warmly greeted. Get this: these two things must be rank-ordered and given some context. They cannot happen simultaneously at the level we hope for. We have to decide. Will we greet our guests? Or will we engage each other in community?

Here's where we've settled at Granger. Have fun when you serve. Do so with people you enjoy. But do it shoulder to shoulder. Never block the guest with your back to them. Keep your stance open so your face and focus are on the guest. Go ahead; chat while you're standing there. But when a guest comes by, shut up. Greet the guest! If you see a guest who needs engagement, leave your friends—cold—and attend to the needs or interests of the guest. Your guests are your priority.

If your team conversation is critical, as in it must happen right now, then leave the floor. If it's that immediate and crucial, excuse yourselves, find replacements, and go elsewhere to talk. Or agree to talk later. Yes, you matter. Yes, your teammates matter. Just don't pretend you can focus fully on each other and your guests at the same time. You can't. You won't.

Wrestle with the tension and make sure your guests are the priority. Bust up your party.

#78 Grab a Friend

Paul wrote in Ephesians 4:3: "Make every effort to keep the unity of the Spirit through the bond of peace." Those are bold, challenging words. Although unity is found in the Holy Spirit, we are to play a significant role keeping it. That doesn't just happen. It requires humility, forgiveness, and hard work.

However, in the church world, we tend to think that this means we'll somehow always click with every individual. We'll be great buds. We'll have endearing relationships with everyone. Hardly! While respect, grace, and love are to be our common practice, we all won't be great friends.

That's not all bad. We're humans with unique personalities. Chemistry matters in relationships; sometimes we just don't hit it off. And yet, we try to push through it. Make it work. Unity doesn't necessarily mean affinity.

Unfortunately, people too often end up leaving teams, upset (or at least disappointed) with not merely their team, but the church. Nuts.

We tell our new guest services team members: "Hey, you may find yourself on a team doing the exact ministry task you love doing. The mission, the work, the focus—it fires you up. You're fulfilled. But at the same time, you find yourself not all that excited. You start to dread showing up to volunteer. That's no good.

"But often it's just because you don't have great chemistry with the people you're serving with. They're fine people. They're moving with the same mission. They're taking steps toward Christ like you are. But you're not clicking. There's no personal chemistry between you.

"That's okay! Tell someone. Tell your leader. Let's help you find a way to serve with people you really enjoy being around! Serving—volunteering—is not merely about the task. It is about relationship, too. We need to work hard to strike that balance."

Jesus looked at his team in John 15 and told them, "I have called you friends."

Grab a friend. Make some new friends. It'll put the fun in service!

#79 | Have Fun!

I grew up in church thinking that being a Christian meant you'd serve, and real service meant sacrifice, and sacrifice meant not having what you wanted, and not having what you wanted meant suffering, and suffering meant you wouldn't always be happy...and apparently not being happy meant you were a Christian. That's messed up. Big time.

Serving, or volunteering, will at times require sacrifice, but enjoying what you do while serving Jesus just might be the point. Serving should produce joy. It should be fun!

When it comes to guest services in the local church, that's precisely why it's not enough to brush your teeth and smile. People can read a fake smile. And they can tell when you're having fun.

Here are three simple reasons to have fun when serving/volunteering in guest services:

- Fun is about joy!
  - ➤ "Be joyful always." (1 Thessalonians 5:16)

- Fun is contagious among your team and your guests!
  - ➤ Years ago in my retail management days, my regional manager told me that if I built a strong team who liked each other and had fun together, I would never have to recruit staff outside of my store again. And he was right! A year or so after assuming management of the store, mall walkers began stopping in to hang out just because they loved the vibe in our store. Customers began to ask me how they could become part of the team— because they witnessed the camaraderie of my staff and the atmosphere in the store (and, yes, they liked the clothes).

- Fun reflects fit!
  - ➤ When people are serving in a way that honors their unique, God-designed wiring, they will have fun! Yes, there will be hard work, but the process, payoff, and relationships will outweigh the

sacrifice. At the end of the day, people who are wired to serve on your teams will have fun.

Have some fun:

- Pick a theme food for the weekend. Everyone bring something to share. Since when wasn't eating fun?
- Give prizes for friends invited to check out the team.
- Throw a party. And keep it social. Singing is great, but you don't have to strike up the band at the bowling alley.
- But you should sing "Happy Birthday" to celebrate a team member's special day.
- Don't take yourself too seriously. Relax. Be real. Laugh at yourself. Set the mood; others will follow.

Get the right people on the team, and give them permission to have fun—your teams will soar, and your guests will benefit!

#80   **Practice Smiling!**

Christians can be some of the most sour, angry-looking people I've met. I've been in some churches where the majority of people don't smile. You'd think the "joy of the Lord" would show up somewhere on their faces, but alas, the joy is as absent as the smile. Sad.

It's particularly sad if your desire is to create a safe, welcoming, and accepting environment in your church that says, "We're glad you're here!" Smiling really should be considered a "best practice."

Keikyu Railways in Tokyo, Japan is intent on making smiling a best practice. In 2009 the company installed software and cameras that grade employees' smiles—on a scale from 0 to 100.

Reporting on the unusual practice, CNN's Morgan Neill wrote: "In the beginning, everyone was confused," says station attendant Kiyomi Ogiwara, "But now it has become a habit. In the morning, everyone lines up and practices smiling."

Along the way, the program offers advice on improving one's smile; for example, "relax" or "breathe deeply." Though the company hasn't laid down firm rules for its use, one idea under consideration would have workers print out a photo of their 100 percent smile and carry it with them so they can consult it throughout the day.

To those who say they would rather have good service than a smile, Keikyu Railways representative Taichi Takahashi replies, "Of course good service is the most important [thing]. But you can't give good service with a scary face. The smile affects overall service."

Your guests recognize fake in a heartbeat. A fake smile doesn't connect with the eyes. When you put on a smile, your mouth curves up, but your eyes have no idea they were supposed to be part of the facial movement. Your heart didn't engage them, any more than it did your mouth. Mere muscles moved, that's it.

There's a door host at a local department store whose job it is to greet customers. I think her job might be to smile, too. And she does.

She doesn't smile as you approach the door, or even as you walk through it. But when your eyes connect with hers, it's there. For a second. It's quick...and fake. It's just a quick flash. A job.

At a neighboring department store is another door host. She's always smiling. Always. When your eyes connect with hers, the smile becomes joyous. She's contagious. Not loud, not attention-seeking, but oh, contagious. (And she looks like Shirley MacLaine. I'm fairly certain she's not channeling; she just looks like her.) I smile when she greets me. I can't help it. I miss her when she's not working.

- What if people are comparing your greeters' smiles to the greeters' smiles at the church down the street? Should they? Should there be any difference?

- What if you were graded on your smile? What if your teams were graded on their smiles? How would you and your teams score?

- Do you think people miss you when you're not there?

How can you make smiling a best practice? Hire a smile coach? Write signs on mirrors? Install hidden cameras? Say "cheese!" a lot? Practice?

How will you perpetuate a contagious, heartfelt, joy-revealing smile?

#81 | It's Not About You

Accept it. It's not about you. Not completely.

After someone has hung around Granger a few weeks, and most certainly when they're ready to help shoulder our mission by joining a team, we tell them this straight up, without apology:

"There probably was a time when it was all about you. The café was about you. The traffic team was about you. The kids' launch zone slides were about you. The stage fog and lights and music were about you. But after you've been around awhile, after you've agreed to join the mission we share, it's not about you. It's about others—others who aren't here yet or who are new to our church.

"After being around a bit, you become a 'regular,' even a member. It's easy to let a sense of entitlement settle in. You can start to wonder 'what's in it for me?' You can wish the music was more your style, or think the café should carry your brand of coffee. But joining the mission of the church isn't about entitlement or comfort. It's about shared responsibility. It's about sacrifice. It's about others. Others who'll take our parking spot, our favorite seat, and the attention of the guest services teams. Yep. That's right. It's not about you. It's about Jesus and the others he died for, too."

As my friend Brian Marshall, connections pastor at Foothills Community Church (Seneca, SC), puts it: "You lose your rights!" He tells his teams, "You get to come early and stay late, sometimes serving people you don't know. And be careful not to pat yourself on the back while you are moving from success to significance!"

Newsbreak: it's not about you.

WORST PRACTICE

When people try to trip you up with "the church is people," just remember you're a "people"! The church owes you! Be reasonable with your serve. Give too much, and people will always expect you to live that way.

#82 | You're Always "On"

You're always "on." Period.

Here's the deal. You're on staff at your church, or you're a faithful volunteer. Either way, you're visible. You may not realize it, but because you serve with any degree of regularity, people at your church know who you are. And they expect you to be real. Consistent. Authentic.

It doesn't matter if you're wearing your "I'm on this weekend" name badge. People still expect you to be kind. They expect you'll still speak, that you'll interact, that you'll care. If those virtues only show up when you wear the guest services label, you're nothing more than a hired hand, not really concerned about the "sheep." (See what Jesus had to say about that in John 10.)

You're always "on."

Even to your newest, first-time guest. They've never seen you before. They don't know you're a greeter, an usher, or a staffer, because you're not wearing your label. You're not "on." But get this: your guest doesn't know that. You're not only *at* the church—you *ARE* the church to this guest. Label or not.

That's the good and the bad news. You get to be real. Consistently loving. Honestly engaged. You don't get to "just come into church with your family." The people you pass and sit next to in the service expect you to be you.

Question is, who are you?

You're "on."

#83 Information Matters

Several years ago, the staff of Village View Church north of Orlando treated my wife and me to a luxurious dinner in The Villages. The restaurant was the Nancy Lopez Legacy Country Club. Great ambience, inviting décor, and delicious food.

When I eat out, I always want to know the server's name. There's a good chance I'll want something during the meal, and I'd rather not call out, "Hey, you!" Plus, when I extend a personal connection to the server, I'm also laying down a service test: Will he/she meet me at that level? Will they serve with genuine care and connect on a human level rather than mere task and a scripted agenda?

That evening, I located the name badge on our server's shirt. Nice touch. It was gold. Impressive. Then I read his name: "Trainee." Not so nice touch. Not impressive. Now, I might just have to yell, "Hey, you!" That would have to be better than "Hey, Trainee!"

The restaurant chose not to partner Mr. Trainee with a visible, nearby Mr. or Ms. Trainer. In my opinion they announced instead, "This guy's new. And we don't want you to remember his name. In fact, there's a chance the experience may be so bad that we'll never get to the point of creating a real name tag for him. He's in a probation period. Thanks for helping us with the test."

Before I sound too much like a hardcore critic and pretentious snob, I should add that when I see someone in training, I pull out some extra grace. I know they're new. I know they will make mistakes and not serve with the same ease and/or timeliness as a comfortable, competent veteran server. I get that.

So when he wasn't sure of the answer to our first question ("What's the fish of the day?"), he went to the kitchen for the answer. I was pleased with his willingness to say, "I don't know, but I'll find out."

However, by the eighth time (no kidding) that he went to the kitchen for the answer, I was losing my patience—not with him, but with the management. This poor man had been hung out to dry. He was ill-informed and under-trained. He didn't know the vegetable of the day, the soup of the day, the fresh catch...essential things to creating an adequate experience for the guest.

This management team may have considered that if he learns by asking, his training experience will be more complete. Maybe. But they failed to consider the experience of the patron who never agreed to be part of the training program. Nor did they consider the frustration and embarrassment for this man who was left feeling incompetent and unprofessional.

It was another great reminder that when our guest services teams in our churches are ill-informed, we hang them out to dry. We frustrate them, because they feel incompetent and unprofessional. And we sabotage the experience of our guests, who leave wondering who's leading the chaos.

I don't live in Florida; if I did, I'm not sure I'd go back to that restaurant.

And I'm sure there are guests in our churches who never return because we don't know our own menu or how to order from it quickly and easily.

Keep your "information specialists" informed. The staff and volunteers who serve in your reception area and guest services center have one primary win: assist your guests by answering questions and providing desired information. If they aren't "in the know," they lose, your guests lose—you lose. It's a no-win situation.

Keeping people well-informed will require intentional systems for communication, promotion, and feedback. Your guests don't really care if the youth department didn't get the info to the front line. They don't care if...(fill in the blank). They just want answers. They need information.

It communicates care and value when systems—technology and people—deliver answers that serve people...and help them take their next step toward Christ.

#84 Create an (i)FAQ Notebook

Here's another best practice from Danny Franks (Summit Church, Durham, North Carolina). He calls it the (i)FAQ Notebook. Here's how he describes it:

> "Our information table volunteers kept getting random questions that we didn't always think to train for: Which campus/service offers interpretation for the deaf? Does the church have a benevolence ministry? Do you offer rides from local college campuses? We collect those questions from volunteers on a weekly basis and update our Infrequently Asked Questions notebook. That notebook also includes a quick fact sheet on each of our major ministries, a weekend-at-a-glance document highlighting information that will be communicated from the stage, and more information that helps them do their job well."

You may want to start by producing a printed FAQ notebook. List the stuff that people are always asking. Document responses and resources that allow your teams to provide consistently accurate information. Then go to work logging every question— the infrequently asked questions.

The greatest value you give your information specialists is accurate and complete information.

It's what you're asking them to do.

I want people who are innately sensitive to the needs, interests, and expectations of our guests. That is, they don't have to work at figuring out what our guests want. It's in their nature, part of their wiring. In part it's because they remember experiences when they've been "Wowed!" They are people who remember their own guest service experiences—both desirable and undesirable. They still cringe when they recall the times they were poorly served. They remember their own disappointment when the service could have been better, when they could have experienced more value and care.

Bring *marketplace customers* onto your team. The reason they remember both great and poor personal experiences is not because they are self-focused consumers. Rather, it's because they understand human value, basic care, and personal service. They get what it is to value people. And when your guests experience that they matter to you and your church, they'll be open to hear that they matter to God.

And isn't that the point?

#86 | Let 'Em Lead

Empower your guest services volunteer leaders to lead. That's what you asked them to do. During training events at Granger, we'll have 20 to 50 volunteers serving our guests. During any given weekend, our guest services volunteers will number more than 100. Volunteer leaders lead those teams. They share the vision that's core to the fabric of our DNA. They understand SHAPE-based ministry (that is—people are uniquely gifted to serve in specific roles). They lead and people follow. We've empowered them with authority and entrusted our teams to their care.

When you ask a leader to lead:

- Make their role clear. Everyone wants to know what a "win" looks like. What do you really expect?
- Give parameters that clarify you're on the same page. It's good to state baseline expectations and outcomes.
- Resource them with space to ask questions, tools to get the job done, and access to people to build the team.
- Check in with them—not to parent, but to support, cheerlead, and partner. Redirect where necessary, and do so with care and respect.
- Pray for them. It'll remind you who is ultimately leading—God.
- Get out of their way. Let them do what you've asked them to do.

All of this assumes that trust, shared vision, mutual respect, and a healthy relationship exist between you and the volunteer leader you've asked to lead. All this can be applied to any leader on any team, in or out of the local church.

Empower the right leaders to serve alongside you, and your guests will be the benefactors. Let 'em lead!

WORST PRACTICE

Don't trust others to lead what you're responsible to lead. Never completely delegate responsibility to others. Especially volunteers. You lead—micro, macro, whatever-o.

#87 | Elevate Servanthood

You've heard it—"It's not my job." "I'm not doin' that!" "I've already put in my time." You've heard it from the clerk at the service station, a customer service rep on the phone...maybe even at church.

Around Granger, we've been making transitions from vocabulary that church people tend to use to vocabulary that everyone understands. Effective communication is about clarity. Clarity is about the primary message getting through. We don't want anything to stand in the way of the message of Jesus, so we're intentionally reviewing our language.

We made shifts like: *volunteer expo* not *ministry fair; community* not *fellowship; next step* not *go deeper.* How we communicate really matters.

However, following all the work to clarify and simplify our language, I found myself in conversations dealing specifically with the difference between *volunteer* and *serve.* Volunteer was one of those preferred words on our list. In fact, you'll notice it on our website. It's common language. It's normal. Everyone knows what it means. And it's an easy first step for anyone. Who doesn't volunteer their time somewhere?

But I don't want people to be around Granger for too long before they begin to be introduced to the concept of serving, rather than simply volunteering. People who merely volunteer can do so with a sense of willingness to "help you out." And that's great! A vision is required for people to volunteer. But the vision for the difference Christ can make in the lives of people requires sacrifice. It requires servants.

I want team members—in guest services or any other team—who willingly see beyond themselves. People who understand that it's not about them; they do what they do to serve—both guests and fellow teammates. People who understand that the message we're striving to make clear is about Jesus—not them. Servants who "get it," who are being changed by the love of Jesus to focus outward toward others.

When servant-hearted people serve, people will know they matter to God...because they'll know they matter to us.

#88 Align Your Teams

You must have people on your teams who embrace and own your mission.

They must value the experience you're creating, the environments you're developing, and the objectives you're accomplishing. When people aren't aligned with who you are, what you're doing and how you're doing it, they will always pull away from your mission, vision, values, and purposes. At Granger, we insist people are fully aligned before they join our first impressions teams.

That said, they may not be Christ-followers yet. While most of the team members who make up our guest services teams are committed Christ-followers, there are a number of places where those who are not yet convinced are invited to serve. However, they must value that the experience, the environment, and the purpose in which our serving occurs is Christ-centered. It's not just a club, not a nice place to be, not merely fun. Rather, we are about creating an experience where people are encouraged to question, explore, and take steps toward Christ...together.

#89 | Shut Up Already

You need people on your teams who are disciplined conversationalists. That is, you need people who know how and when to shut up already. A disciplined conversationalist intuitively knows how to carry on a conversation with others without feeling like the conversation has to be all about them.

You've met, and probably know well, someone who is not a disciplined conversationalist. Maybe you're married to one (that's rough). These folks really are great talkers. They're not afraid to open dialogue; they know how. They start conversations with strangers; they know no strangers. They have no problem talking to people. However, they lack the discipline to simply be quiet and listen.

They talk *to* people, not *with* them. They can be highly entertaining, but often not engaging. They tend to focus on people—too often, themselves. In spite of that fact, these folks really do love people, and they're generally well-intended. But, like all of us, the person they know best and feel most comfortable talking about is "me."

It's not a surprise to discover one day that you've somehow brought people like this onto the team. Remember, this is about the guests, so who serves them really matters. How do you make sure your guests are cared for in a gracious manner?

- Do your best to get to know every person joining your team before you invite them to serve.
  - ➢ If not you, then other responsible leaders should discover this kind of tendency before new team members come on board. Early detection is best. Then you either never bring the person on the team or you take time to coach them before you do.

- If you missed the first step already, you'll need to confront the issue—soon.
  - ➢ Behavior that is tolerated is condoned with silence. The sooner you have the conversation, the better your chance of redeeming

the situation. Put it off, and more guests will be turned off...and you'll have little to talk about, since time will have convinced this person that everything is okay.

- When you do confront, deal with the problem and love the person.
  - ➤ Remember, people matter—including this person who may be making your guests feel uncomfortable. This person probably really loves people. They may struggle with a sense of security and try to compensate. They may simply be overusing a self-disclosing skill (used sparingly and with discernment, self-disclosure can reveal both empathy and vulnerability, engaging others in meaningful conversation) and be unaware of their pattern. Whether or not they continue to serve on your team, they want and need to serve somewhere. Help them find an appropriate place to connect.

- Your team needs you to deal with this issue, too.
  - ➤ Your guests are not the only ones impacted by the undisciplined, me-focused greeter. Greeters who serve alongside this person are impacted as well. If it persists, you risk being perceived as aloof and ignorant to what's happening with your guests. Or the team may sense that you're as frustrated as they are, but you're doing nothing about it. Your credibility as a leader is on the line.

I want people on my team who know how to engage people, honor safe personal boundaries, and show a genuine interest in others. Guests can see right through self-centeredness. When our guests look at our team members, I want them to see Jesus. I want them to know they matter to God.

Who's serving on your team? Who needs to learn to shut up already?

#90 | Train Your Teams

The need to train your teams doesn't assume they're incompetent or clueless. If your people *are* incompetent or clueless, they may be volunteering in the wrong area. People who are wired to create a welcoming atmosphere for your guests have an intuitive sense for treating people well. They are people-people, after all.

You can't train personality. You can't train common sense. You can't train giftedness. You *can*, however, call out the best in personality. You *can* inform common sense. You *can* hone giftedness.

So once you have the "right" people on your team, train for these reasons:

- *Remove assumptions.* Even though you have the "right" people on your team doesn't mean that everyone has reached their apex in treating guests excellently. Don't assume.

- *Communicate vision.* People may understand what to do. They need to hear again why.

- *Establish your "brand."* Create consistency in how you treat and respond to your guests.

- *Inform.* Make sure everyone on the team has been equipped with information, allowing them to answer questions and assist your guests.

- *Identify best practices.* Excellence occurs when best practices are identified, communicated, and practiced. Not by a few people, but by the entire team.

- *Get buy-in.* You need everyone on the team to agree with the expectations and norms of the team. Misaligned team members are like a misaligned car. It's a pain to keep in the middle of the road. You're constantly working to adjust the direction and spend too much time doing so.

What your training looks like will vary from church to church. Here are some quick ideas to get you started:

- *Serve food.* Chips and salsa. A full meal. Dessert. Feed them and they will come. It's true.

- *Invite experts.* You may have customer service experts in your church who are leading businesses and/or training in the marketplace. Tap their experience. Let them help you.

- *Role play.* Develop scenarios that your people will encounter. Ask them to play it out. Coach them. Call out best practices. Suggest alternative responses.

- *Keep it simple.* Present a short outline. Make it memorable. Ask: could anyone repeat this to a peer? For a short training outline, check out chapter seven of *First Impressions: Creating Wow Experiences in Your Church* (Group Publishing). You can download this chapter for free at group.com/bonus.

WORST PRACTICE

Bring people onto your teams who get it. If you have to train someone to say "hello," you'll likely have to teach them how to brush their teeth, too.

- *Don't merely train technique; repeat the vision.* There will be time to train and re-train the "what." Vision must be repeated; it's what fuels and motivates.

- *Do most of your training on the job and just in time.* That is, away from the "training event." Most of what needs to stick will find stickiness in the moment.

#91 Choose Interesting

Yes, this is extremely subjective. For instance, after reading this book for a few pages you may not find me all that interesting. Who, after all, gets to decide if someone else is interesting? What are the criteria for determining how interesting any one of us is?

Try this approach. Think about the last time you went to a service, a party, or a sporting event where you personally met someone new, someone interesting. After you went home, you were still thinking about them. In a good way. Perhaps some of these things happened for you:

- You told someone else about them.
- You found yourself wondering when you might bump into them again.
- You sensed that they thought you mattered.
- You wanted to learn more about them.
- You enjoyed their sense of humor.
- You appreciated their demeanor—confident or humble or jovial or sensitive—you liked their personality.

Even if you didn't hear their life story or meet their extended family or flip through their high school yearbook, you found them interesting. You were drawn to them, for whatever reason.

Interesting people.

They will help your guests feel warmly accepted. They will bring a sense of aliveness to your team and culture. They will allow your guests to go home sensing they met someone who genuinely cared, who would be great to know better...someone they'd love to return to your church to see again.

You need interesting people on your guest services team.

#92 | Re-Up

Maybe you noticed. On Tuesday, February 26, 2008 every U.S. Starbucks store (except licensed locations in grocery stores, airports, etc.) closed for three hours to train and celebrate the brand with their baristas (who, by the way, are considered "partners").

With that corporate-wide move, Howard Schultz demonstrated his commitment to turning the company's falling sales numbers around. He began doing so by not merely closing failing stores, but by reminding partners of their first priority to be a community's place for gathering, conversation, and, yes, coffee.

Below is his letter to Starbucks' partners the day prior to the national "closed for training" day. As you read, ask yourself:

- How is our church providing a third place to our people?
- How committed are we to preserving and improving that space?
- What will we do to help our "partners," our volunteers and staff, embrace our core mission and commitment to help people know they matter to God?

Here's a portion of that letter:

> *February 25, 2008*
>
> *To: All Partners*
> *From: Howard Schultz*
> *Re: As we embark on Espresso Excellence Training*
>
> *Tomorrow evening, we will come together in an unprecedented event in our company's storied history. We will close all of our U.S. company-operated stores to teach, educate and share our love of coffee, and the art of espresso. And in doing so, we will begin to elevate the Starbucks Experience for our customers...And we will revisit our standards of quality that*

are the foundation for the trust that our customers have in our coffee and in all of us.

We are the coffee that brings people together every day around the world to foster conversation and community.

Thank you in advance for embracing tomorrow night in the spirit in which it is intended. Have fun, but also make it matter. Learn, teach, and share with your fellow partners.

Onward,

Howard

(Read Howard's complete memorandum at news.starbucks.com/article_display.cfm?article_id=63)

Now, hit the pause button.

- Are you still on mission?
- Is everyone trained?
- What would your letter to your team sound like?
- How will you nail consistency?

#93 Ask for Help

Leaders can get really hung up trying to "prove" their leadership. This is usually not about incompetence. Sadly, most of the time it's about a sense of insecurity. Man up! Get over yourself. Leaders who have something to prove tend to command orders, own every original idea, promote themselves, and avoid asking for help from others. Lead that way very long, and you'll be on a lonely walk.

Secure, competent leaders ask for help. There are plenty of reasons to ask for help:

- You need to shore up weaknesses (you have them, and everyone else knows it).
- You can't see or know everything, and frankly, you don't "own" the ministry.
- Your team members are the grassroots practitioners. They hear comments, they initiate best practices in the moment, and they see flaws in processes and systems. In short, they often have their finger on the pulse of what it really takes to meet guests where they are.

Ask them. Ask them for help. Give them permission to submit ideas for improvement. Solicit their advice. Ask them to share feedback.

And then, listen. Keep listening. Ask questions so you understand. Then listen some more. They are your first "customer," your best eyes, ears, and touch to the rest of your "customers." Listen. Then, with their help, implement change that does more than validate your team. Implement change that best serves your guests in the context of your values and mission.

Ask for help.

#94 | Send a Four-Point Report

Best practices can be produced in a boardroom. *Respond to questions within 48 hours. Answer the phone before the fourth ring. Do what you do with excellence.* But not all best practices can be planned in advance.

Most best practices come in the moment. A one-time occurrence from one team member that gets discovered and repeated. That's what happened with our guest services four-point report.

Our volunteer usher leaders began to e-mail each other following each weekend of services. By Monday afternoon an e-mail was circulating, celebrating highlights and asking questions about how to solve a challenge that had popped up. The e-mail created conversation that birthed an ongoing best-practice-making machine. The Four-Point E-mail was born. It's this simple:

1. Share a highlight from the weekend. Anything positive counts. A story about a guest interaction. A high point from the service itself. A nugget from a team member.

2. Tell about a challenge the team encountered and how it was solved (if one existed at all).

3. Tell about a challenge the team encountered that you still need help with. You dealt with it as best as you could, but ultimately you know a long-term solution is still needed.

4. Finally, share the name of an up-and-coming leader. Everyone will pray for that person and for the leaders who will be pouring into him/her.

WORST PRACTICE

Volunteers give a great portion of their weekend away as they serve. Don't exasperate them with e-mails, phone calls, or visits between serving times. If you can't say it on the weekend, it doesn't need to be said.

This four-point e-mail keeps the communication going well past the weekend. Weekend teams are not isolated; they are united. Unique approaches are not limited to any one leader; they are shared. Best practices are not protected by a team; they are celebrated and practiced by the entire ministry.

#95 Vision as Praise

Everyone needs a cheerleader. But most people need more than that. Cheering happens with a "way to go!" or a "you're awesome," even a "thanks so much!" But if you are responsible for cheering for people, you need to do more.

People need the "why" behind the "thank you." They need to be reminded of the vision, too. Watch the subtle but profound difference in these two comments to a volunteer greeter:

1. "Bob, thanks so much for carving time to serve today! I appreciate it so much!"

2. "Bob, your willingness to be here communicates such value to our guests. Your smile, your encouragement, present Jesus to people who need to know how much they matter to him. Thank you!"

With very few additional words, the second encouragement communicates vision to Bob. Yes, he's been praised and thanked, but he's also been reminded of the "why" behind what he is doing.

Say "thank you," but do so with vision!

#96 | Identify Quality People

Seriously. Have you experienced incompetence behind the counter of a discount department store lately (company names withheld to protect the guilty)? Have you been on the customer side of a sad, grouchy door greeter? Not everyone has the qualities needed for customer service—or guest services, or first impressions ministry, or whatever you call it in your church. You must identify and invite people with appropriate qualities to serve on your guest services teams.

Here's a short definition of "quality":

- Actually like other people
- Smile naturally
- Warm and welcoming
- Sharp, clean appearance
- Able to carry on conversation with someone "new"
- Coachable
- Hospitable
- Joyful

Warm bodies won't cut it. Willing servants aren't enough. From what I see of Peter in the Scriptures, he may have been a disciple of Jesus, but he didn't have the qualities needed to make the cut on my team.

Choose carefully. Choose quality.

#97 Make Everyone a Host

Okay, perhaps you can't make everyone a host; but everyone on your guest services teams should see themselves as a host. At Granger, we still have a number of different labels to distinguish one role from another. For instance, we have ushers, campus guides, and traffic teams (to name a few). However, if people are too narrowly tied to their roles, then after guides guide and traffic teams direct and ushers ush (that is what they do, right?), they are done. They will have completed their task —which is great! It's what they were asked to do.

On the other hand, this thinking produces a frightening amount of potential for your teams to say "that's not my job." That's the last thing you want to hear.

Consider what might happen if everyone on your team saw themselves as a host. Hosts don't merely find seats, guide guests, or park cars. Hosts ensure that every guest has a high-value experience. In the parking lot, around the building, in the service. The role of host doesn't end with a job description or a window of time. Hosts are always...

- alert, looking for opportunities to help guests.
- team players, stepping beyond their label to serve someone else.
- partnering with other teammates to create the best guest experience possible.
- "on," not confined by a window of time, but serving till all guests have been served.

What would it look like if your team played "host"?

#98 | Vision. Repeat. Repeat. Repeat.

You've heard this. John Maxwell has written about it. Bill Hybels, Mark Beeson, and Andy Stanley have taught it. You've communicated it. You know this.

Do it again. Cast the vision.

Vision isn't merely what you're doing. Vision answers the question "Why are we doing this?" It's the "why" behind the "what." Vision is the "so what." It's the reason we do what we do.

And people forget. As soon as you say it again, they know they've known it. But they forgot. Maybe only briefly, but they forgot. And they'll forget again.

And so will we.

So get clear on your vision. Why is it you're doing what you're doing? Then say it again. And again. And again.

- Include it in your reminder postcards.

- Say it as you start meetings.

- Bring it up in hallway conversations.

- Visualize it with videos.

- Tell stories.

- Point it out in someone when you see it.

- Keep it simple.

- Write it out for yourself.

- Find new ways to say it.

- Then say it again.

#99 | Be Healthy

I have a few friends who not only call out the best in my leadership, but they understand that leadership comes from within. Leadership is about who I am, not merely what I do. Some of those friends I connect with daily. Others a few times over several months. And some are across several state lines.

One of those buddies is Brian Marshall. He serves at Foothills Community Church in Seneca, SC. I asked Brian about best practices in his ministry, and he e-mailed me the following:

"The number-one best practice is BE HEALTHY. As a person it is critical to face the 'stuff' in your life. If you don't allow God to be everything, your ministry and life will always be influenced by the unhealthiness. You can't give away what you don't have! Learn to live a holy life, be the example, do the hard work."

Brian gets it. And every time we talk, he speaks from a place of personal integrity, deep dependency on Jesus, and gratitude for God's overwhelming faithfulness. Brian inspires me to be healthy.

"P.S.—You won't be healthy in a vacuum. Find a friend. Be intentional. Ask the hard questions about the 'stuff' in your life. You can only give fully as you allow God to fill you."

#100 | Create a V.I.P. Space

Volunteers are Very Important People, but my friends Brian Marshall (Foothills Community Church, Seneca, South Carolina) and Stacey Windover (West Ridge Church, Dallas, Georgia) insist on creating space for Vision, Information, and Prayer.

We've done the same thing at Granger Community. Any church, any budget, any size can create this space. It's two-fold.

1. This space is physical. It could be a "green room," a reserved classroom, or a hallway. Your teams know where the gathering happens. It's consistent week to week; it's expected that everyone shows up.

2. It's also space created in the schedule. Some of our teams at Granger meet 90 minutes prior to services. Others meet 20 to 30 minutes early. Stacey observes that at West Ridge, "We want team members to leave Volunteer Central feeling cared for, informed, and focused on the vision of helping to lead people on a life-changing journey to follow Jesus Christ."

Require everyone to arrive early enough to meet with the rest of their team for vision, information, and prayer. You'll communicate value to your team members and prepare them to be present and focused on your guests.

#101 Create Your Own Best Practices

This book started with the observation that best practices don't last forever, because in a thriving organization, people continue to find better ways of doing things. Additionally, best practices are often contextualized, developed based on unique needs and opportunities within your church, ministry, or organization.

I've written about 101 best practices, but I certainly didn't create them all. They've come from other leaders I respect, Granger Community Church volunteers, and other churches. But these are not the only best practices.

You have people on your teams who are creating best practices, but no one's written them down. Observe. Make notes. Invite ownership. Challenge your teams to compare behaviors. Compile your own list of best practices—and keep adding to it. You'll take your guest services to new levels of excellence. You'll carry the love of Jesus in fresh ways. And you'll communicate over and over again, "people matter." They matter to God, and they matter to his people.

Mark has spent the past 25 years serving and leading people. While many of those years were focused within the local church, he brings marketplace experience from retail management, as well as career development and training. Regardless of his work or ministry context, he is about investing in people, because he believes people really matter. Think of him as a "people advocate."

He is a unifying force at Granger Community Church, where he oversees adult relational connections, including groups, guest services, and volunteer strategies. As Granger's chief guest services practitioner, he specializes in establishing, inspiring, and cultivating teams of volunteers who make GCC a relaxed, rejuvenating, and relevant experience for members and guests. The teams he builds are passionate about helping people connect with and serve others. Mark also serves as regional site pastor for Granger's Elkhart multi-site location.

Mark's first book, *First Impressions: Creating Wow Experiences in Your Church* (Group), addresses the issues of guest attendance, growth, and volunteer development, offering strategies for making high-impact first impressions. A sought-after consultant and trainer, Mark has helped local churches of all sizes improve their guest services experience.

Mark's vision extends well beyond Granger's weekend services; he is the driving force behind the church's commitment to helping people discover their unique significance to serve in the 200+ volunteer roles at GCC. His book *Lasting Impressions: From Visiting to Belonging* (Group) picks up where *First Impressions* leaves off. With practical insight and honest stories, Mark presents a strategy for creating environments that encourage people to own their journey in personal relationships, helping them belong to, not merely attend, church.

His clear understanding of guests, expertise in team-building, and keen eye for excellence call out the best in the people who make up the local church—any local church. Mark serves and leads because people matter.

Mark shares his love of life and people with Laura, his wife of nearly 30 years, and their teenage daughter, Olivia.

Order these other great titles by Mark Waltz!

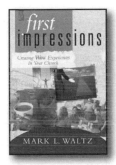

First Impressions:
Creating Wow Experiences In Your Church
Mark Waltz

Before a service even begins, first-time guests usually decide whether they'll return to your church. This means church leaders need to create no-fail, practical ways to ensure a visitor's first impression is the best impression. Author Mark Waltz shares the strategies that work in his church—and takes "greeting" to a whole new level.

When guests feel valued, they will return. And when they do, they'll have the opportunity to experience Jesus' love. Let visitors know "You matter to God, so you matter to us."

▶ ISBN 978-0-7644-2757-2 $19.99

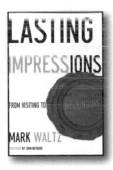

Lasting Impressions:
From Visiting to Belonging
Mark Waltz

If Christians were cars, most would be recalled. That's because the vast majority of Christians aren't going anywhere. They aren't taking the next steps in their spiritual journey. They're stalled. This practical guide addresses that dilemma, offering a proven strategy for turning church guests into believers, and believers into committed Christ-followers. The model offered by author Mark Waltz is flexible and adaptable for any congregation.

▶ ISBN 978-0-7644-3747-2 $19.99